CHAMPIONSHIP FIGHTING

*Explosive Punching
and
Aggressive Defense*

JACK DEMPSEY

Simon & Schuster

New York   London   Toronto   Sydney   New Delhi

Simon & Schuster
1230 Avenue of the Americas
New York, NY 10020

First Simon & Schuster trade paperback edition January 2015

SIMON & SCHUSTER and colophon are registered trademarks
of Simon & Schuster, Inc.

For information about special discounts for bulk purchases,
please contact Simon & Schuster Special Sales at 1-866-506-1949
or business@simonandschuster.com.

The Simon & Schuster Speakers Bureau can bring authors to
your live event. For more information or to book an event contact
the Simon & Schuster Speakers Bureau at 1-866-248-3049 or visit
our website at www.simonspeakers.com.

Cover portrait by Cassidy J. Alexander © 1983 by Centerline Press

Printed in Canada

20 19 18

ISBN 978-1-5011-1148-8

Contents

Chapter 1: Explosives at Toledo

WHAT would happen if a year-old baby fell from a fourth-floor window on to the head of a burly truck driver, standing on the sidewalk?

It's practically certain that the truckman would be knocked unconscious. He might die of brain concussion or a broken neck. Even an innocent little baby can become a dangerous missile *when its body-weight is set into fast motion*.

You may feel as helpless as a year-old infant—as far as fighting is concerned; but please remember: (1) *You weigh more than a baby,* and (2) *You need not fall from a window to put your body-weight into motion.* You have weight, and you have the means of launching that weight into fast motion. Furthermore, you have *explosive* ingredients. You may not appear as harmless as a stick of dynamite, which children have been known to mistake for an oversized stick of taffy. You can launch your body-weight into fast motion; and, like dynamite, you can *explode* that hurtling weight against an opponent with a stunning, blasting effect known as *follow-through*.

Incidentally, mention of the baby and explosives reminds me of what happened at Toledo on the afternoon of July 4, 1919. Standing there that day under the blazing Ohio sun, I felt like a baby as I glanced across the ring and saw big Jess Willard shrug off his bathrobe in the opposite corner. Cowboy Jess was heavyweight champion of the world, and he was a giant. Moreover, he was a perfectly proportioned giant. He was every inch an athlete. He tapered down beautifully from derrick-like shoulders, and his muscles were so smooth you could scarcely see them

7

rippling under his sun-tanned skin. He towered six feet, six inches and a quarter. He weighed 245 pounds. In comparison I shaped up like an infant or a dwarf although I nudged past six feet and scaled 180 pounds. My weight was announced as 187 pounds; but actually I registered only 180.

As I looked across the ring at Willard, I said to myself, " Jeez! What a mountain I've got to blast down this time!"

I knew about blasting—about dynamite. I had learned about dynamite in the mines of Colorado, Utah and Nevada, where I had worked off and on for about six years. And I knew plenty about dynamite in fighting. I had made a study of fistic dynamite since I was seven years old. That was when I had my first fist-fight, with a boy about my own size, in Manassa, Colorado. I was born at Manassa and spent my early years there.

Before I fought Willard, my manager (Doc) Kearns—already had nicknamed me " Jack the Giant-Killer " because I had belted out such big fellows as Carl Morris and Fred Fulton. They were big men all right, but neither had appeared such an awesome giant as Willard did that sweltering afternoon. I had trained for Willard at the Overland Club on Maumee Bay, an inlet of Lake Erie. Nearly every day Kearns and Trainer Jimmy Deforest reported that I was shaping up much better than Willard. But when I saw big Jess across the ring, without an ounce of fat on his huge frame, I wondered if Kearns and Deforest had been bringing me pleasant but false reports to bolster my courage. I won't say I was scared as I gazed at Willard, but I'll admit I began to wonder if I packed enough dynamite to blast the man-mountain down.

Since this is not a story of my life, I'll refrain from boring you with details of the fight. I'll wrap it up in a hurry; I'll merely recall that I sent Jess crashing to the canvas six or seven times in the first round and gave him such a battering in the third session that Jess was unable to come out for the fourth round. As Willard sat helplessly on his stool in

8

the corner, his handlers threw in the towel just after the bell had rung to start the fourth. I won the world heavy-weight championship on a technical knockout. I won the ring's most coveted title by stopping a man much larger and stronger than I was—one who outweighed me 65 pounds. I blasted him into helplessness by exploding my fast-moving body-weight against him. I used body-weight, with which the falling baby could knock out the truck driver; and I used explosion.

Exploding body-weight is the most important weapon in fist-fighting or in boxing. Never forget that! I was at my peak as a fighter the day I met Willard under the broiling Toledo sun. My body-weight was moving like lightning, and I was exploding that weight terrifically against the giant. Even before the first round was finished, Willard looked like the victim of a premature mine blast.

Chapter 2: Good and Bad Toledo Aftermaths

THE explosives I displayed against Willard were harnessed soon by Promoter Tex Rickard to produce five gates of more than $1,000,000 each. Those receipts were genuinely remarkable; for when Willard and I drew $452,224 at Toledo, that was the largest fight-gate on record. My five big-money bouts were with Georges Carpentier of France, Luis Angel Firpo of Argentina, Jack Sharkey of Boston, and Gene Tunney of New York (two).

Because I was a good puncher and because each opponent in those five big-gate fights was a hard-hitter, the tremendous publicity given those extravanganzas made the world more punch-conscious than ever before. Incidentally, don't let anyone tell you Gene Tunney couldn't punch. Many fight fans have that wrong impression today. In our first bout at Philadelphia, where Gene wrested the title from me, he landed a right-counter to the head that staggered me early in the first round. I didn't recover fully from that punch during the rest of the fight. And at Chicago, in our second scrap, Gene drove me to one knee with a head-blow in the eighth round. Mind you, that was after I'd floored him for the "long count" in the seventh. Indeed, I found Gentleman Gene surprisingly explosive.

Since those golden Rickard-Dempsey days, the public's worship of punch has become more intense; for interest in the kayo sock has been stimulated increasingly by press, radio and television. And that intense public interest in punch has been one admirable aftermath of the blasting in Toledo. In addition, those big gates gave lads everywhere the desire to become good punchers so that they, too, might hammer out riches with their fists. Those two effects—public worship of punch and youngsters' desire to hit hard—would have had a most beneficial influence upon the science of self-defence, were it not for an unexpectedly blighting development.

Unfortunately, my big gates did more to commercialize fighting than anything else in pugilistic history. They transformed boxing into a big-time business. As a commercial enterprise, the fight-game began attracting people who knew little or nothing about self-defence. Hoping to make quick money, they flocked into boxing from other fields. They came as promoters, managers, trainers and even instructors. Too often they were able to crowd out old-timers because they had money to invest, because they were better businessmen, or merely because they were glib-talking hustlers. They joined the gold rush in droves—dentists, doctors, lawyers, restaurant proprietors, clothing manufacturers, butchers, grocers, bookies, racket guys, and pool-hall hangers-on. Fellows who never tossed a fist in their lives became trainers. They mistaught boys in gymnasiums. Those mistaught youths became would-be fighters for a while; and when they hung up their gloves, they too became instructors.

It was only natural that the tide of palooka experts should sweep into the amateur ranks, where lack of knowledge among instructors today is as pathetic as among professional handlers. And that's not the worst. Too many amateur instructors have forgotten entirely that the purpose of boxing lessons is to teach a fellow to defend himself with his fists; not to point him toward amateur or professional competition with boxing gloves. To a menacing extent the major purpose of fistic instruction has been by-passed by amateur tutors who try to benefit themselves financially, indirectly or directly, by producing punchless performers who can win amateur or professional bouts on points.

Not one youth in fifty has any ambitions to become a

professional fighter when he first goes to an instructor. That's particularly true among college and high-school lads. Yet the instructors continue—teaching boys to become "smart" boxers instead of well-rounded fighters. And that's a downright shame, for punch is absolutely essential in fist-fighting and it's an invaluable asset in amateur or professional boxing. Actually, it's *stupid* instead of *smart* instruction to teach other fighting movements to a boy before he has been taught to punch.

Because of this commercial, win-on-a-point-as-soon-as-possible attitude among modern instructors, the amateur and professional ranks today are cluttered with futile "club fighters" and "fancy Dans." In the professional game there are so few genuine fighters that promoters find it almost impossible to make enough attractive matches to fill their boxing dates.

At this writing lack of worthwhile talent in the heavyweight division is particularly appalling. It's almost unbelievable that the heavy division should have declined so far since the days when I was fighting my way up in 1917, 1918 and 1919. The class was jammed with good men then. Jess Willard was champion. On his trail were Carl Morris, Frank Moran, Bill Brennan, Billy Miske, Fred Fulton, Homer Smith, Gunboat Smith, Jim Flynn and Porky Flynn. And there were Sam Langford, Harry Wills, Tommy Gibbons and Willie Meehan. With the exception of fat Meehan, any one of those top-fighters could knock your brains out if you made a mistake while facing him. Meehan, although a slapper, threw so much leather and was so rugged that he and I broke even in our three four-round bouts. I won, we drew, and I lost.

Lack of top-notchers in the heavy division and in most other divisions today reflects the scarcity of good instructors and trainers everywhere. There are a few good ones lingering on, but they are notable exceptions. Joe Louis found a good instructor when he was about sixteen. He found Atler

Ellis at the Brewster Centre in Detroit. Ellis, an old-time fighter, taught Joe how to punch and how to box. And when Joe turned professional, he went immediately under the wing of the late Jack Blackburn, grand old-time fighter and one of the finest trainers the ring ever produced. Joe developed into an accurate explosive " sharpshooter " who could " take you out " with either fist. He was a great champion.

Chapter 3 : Punchers Are Made; Not Born

Louis retired as undefeated heavyweight champion in 1949. And I'll bet that, as he retired, Joe considered himself a natural-born puncher. I know that's probably true because I had the same mistaken idea about myself during my career and for a time after I hung up my gloves.

If you're a punching champion it's natural for you to get the wrong appreciation of yourself. Hundreds of admirers pat you on the back and tell you what a " natural-born " fighter you are. And when you're swept along toward seventh heaven by the roar of the crowd in your magnificent moments of triumph, it's easy to forget the painstaking labour with which you and your instructors and trainers and sparring partners fashioned each step in your stairway to the throne. It's easy to forget the disappointments and despair that, at times, made the uncompleted stairway seem like " Heartbreak Hill." Ah yes, when you're on the throne, it's easy to regard yourself as one who was *born* to the royalty of the ring.

In your heyday as champion, you can't " see the forest for the trees." As an historian might express it, you're too close to your career to get the proper perspective of highlights and background. It was only after I had retired and had begun trying to teach others how to fight that I investigated the steps in my stairway—analyzed my own technique. And that was a tough job. You see: by the time a fellow becomes a successful professional fighter, nearly all his moves are so instinctive, through long practice, that it's difficult for him to sort out the details of each move. Accordingly, it is nearly impossible—at first—for him to explain his moves to a beginner. He can say to the beginner, "you throw a straight right like this." Then he can shoot a straight right at a punching bag. But the beginner will have no more conception of how to punch with the right than he had before. That's the chief reason why so few good fighters developed into good instructors. They failed to go back and examine each little link in each boxing move. They tried to give their pupils the chains without the links.

When I began breaking down my moves for the purpose of instruction, I found it most helpful to swing my memory clear back to the days when I was a kid at Manassa, a small town in southern Colorado. I was fortunate as a kid. My older brothers, Bernie and Johnny, were professional fighters. They had begun teaching me self-defence by the time I was seven years old. In my break-down, I tried to recall exact details of the first fundamentals my brothers taught me. I jotted down every detail of those instructions I could remember, and every detail that dawned on me while I was practising those early fundamentals. Then I moved mentally across the Great Divide to Montrose, Colorado, the town where I spent my later youth. There was more interest in fighting in Montrose than in any place of its size I've ever known. It was a town of would-be fighters. In some Montrose families there were four or five brothers who wanted to be fighters. I found plenty of kid sparmates there and plenty of instructors—some good, some bad.

My investigation of technique took me on a long mental journey as I followed my fighting trail through the West, where I had worked at any job I could get in mines, lumber camps, hash-houses, on ranches, etc. I was fighting on the side in those days, and I was getting pointers on self-defence from all the old-timers I met. Each trainer, each manager, each fighter had his own ideas and his own specialities. Like a blotter on legs, I absorbed all that information in those days, and then discarded what seemed wrong.

Swinging back through Memory Lane, I found myself, at twenty-one, making my first trip to New York, where I fought Andre Anderson, "Wild Bert" Kenny and John Lester Johnson, who cracked two of my ribs. Although that New York trip was a disappointment, I received much valuable fighting information from top-flight heavies like Frank Moran, Bill Brennan, Billy Miske and Gunboat Smith, when each dropped into Grupp's Gymnasium. And I recalled the details of my later post-graduate courses in fighting from Doc Kearns and Trainer Deforest, one of the best instructors in the world. Deforests's career went clear back to the days of Peter Jackson and London prize-ring rules.

That geographic investigation of my own technique really humbled me. It hit me right on the chin with the booming fact that since I was seven years old, I'd had the opportunity to learn punching from a long parade of guys who had studied it. I had absorbed their instructions, their pointers, their theories, in Manassa, Montrose, Provo, Ogden, Salt Lake City, Goldfield, Tonopah, New York, San Francisco, Chicago, St. Paul, and many other cities—before I met Willard at Toledo. And let me emphasize that in the days when I was drinking in all that information, the fighters, trainers and managers knew much more about punching than they generally know today. You must remember that when I fought Willard in 1919, it was only twenty-seven years after Jim Corbett had beaten John L. Sullivan at New Orleans in the first championship fight with big gloves. While I was coming up, the technique of the old masters was still fresh in the minds of fighting men. Now, it is thirty years since the day I fought Willard. During those thirty years fighting became "big business"; but in the scramble for money in the cauliflower patch, the punching technique of the old masters—Sullivan, Corbett, Bob Fitzsimmons, Tommy Ryan, Joe Gans, Terry McGovern, and others— seems to have been forgotten.

Chapter 4: Why I Wrote This Book

NATURALLY, I didn't make the detailed exploration of my fighting past all at one sitting. I'm a restless guy; I don't like to sit long in one place. But I became so interested in the work that sometimes I'd spend an hour or two hours at it. I did it on trains, in planes, in hotel rooms, and at home.

Max Waxman, my business manager, used to say, "For cryin' out loud, Jack, what are you writin' down all that junk for? You're supposed to be a memory expert. You must have all that dope about fightin' right in your own head. Seems silly to see you sweatin' and fumin' and writin' notes about stuff you got at your fingertips."

Well, the log of my mental journey from Manassa to Toledo, filled 384 pages with closely-written notes in long-hand. I'm confident those 384 pages represented the most thorough study ever made by any prominent fighter of his own technique and of the pointers he had received first-hand from others.

But my job had only begun. I spent several months study-ing that mass of information and separating it into the different departments of self-defence—under sections, sub-sections, sub-sub-sections, etc., I waded through it again and again. I combed it; I sieved it; I sluice-boxed it for details I needed in each smallest sub-sub-section. And then, into each slot I dropped any additional knowledge I had gained since Toledo. Those different departments, with their various minor brackets, gave me for the first time a clear panorama of self-defence.

I was pretty proud of my panorama. I was confident at

last that I could take the rawest beginner, or even an experienced fighter, and teach him exactly what self-defence was *all* about. Then I became curious to compare my panorama with those of other men in boxing. I talked to many fighters, trainers and instructors; and I read every book on boxing I could buy. My conversations and my reading left me utterly amazed at the hazy, incomplete and distorted conceptions of self-defence possessed by many who are supposed to be experts. Perhaps I was unjustly critical. Perhaps none of them had had my unusual opportunities to get a blueprint that mapped all the fundamentals, at least. Or perhaps they took many fundamentals for granted and did not include them in their explanations.

At any rate, I came to the conclusion that self-defence is being taught wrong nearly everywhere, for the following major reasons:

1. Beginners are not grounded in the four principal methods of putting the body-weight in fast motion: (a) *falling step*, (b) *leg spring*, (c) *shoulder whirl*, (d) *upward surge*.

2. The extremely important *power line* in punching seems to have been forgotten.

3. The wholesale failure of instructors and trainers to appreciate the close co-operation necessary between the *power line* and *weight-motion* results generally in *impure punching*—weak hitting.

4. Explosive straight punching has become almost a *lost art* because instructors place so much *emphasis on shoulder whirl* that beginners are taught wrongfully to punch straight *without stepping* whenever possible.

5. Failure to teach the *falling step* ("trigger step") for straight punching has resulted in the *left jab* being used generally as a light, auxiliary weapon for making openings and "setting up," instead of as a *stunning blow*.

6. Beginners are not shown the difference between *shovel hooks* and *uppercuts*.

7. Beginners are not warned that taking *long steps* with hooks may open up those hooks into *swings*.

8. The *bob-weave* rarely is explained properly.

9. Necessity for the *three-knuckle landing* is never pointed out.

10. It is my personal belief that *beginners should be taught all types of punches before being instructed in defensive moves*, for nearly every defensive move should be accompanied by a simultaneous or a delayed counterpunch. You *must* know how to punch and you must have punching confidence before you can learn aggressive defence.

My dissatisfaction with current methods of teaching self-defence was the principal reason why I decided to put my panorama into a book. I realized, too, that my explosive performances and big gates in the "Golden Decade" were indirectly responsible for current unsatisfactory methods; so, it was my duty to lend a helping hand. Moreover, it's my impression now that thousands of boys and men throughout the world would grasp eagerly at the chance to learn how to use their fists—how to become knockout punchers in a hurry.

Never before has there been such need for self-defence among fellows everywhere as there is today. Populations increased so rapidly during the past quarter-century, while improved methods in transportation shrank the globe, that there is much crowding now. Also the pace of living has been so stepped-up that there is much more tension in nearly every activity than there was in the old days.

Crowding, pace, and tension cause friction, flare-ups, angry words and blows. That unprecedented friction can be noted particularly in cities, where tempers are shortened by traffic jams, sidewalk bumpings, crowdings in subways and on buses, and jostlings in theatres, saloons and night-clubs.

Chapter 5: Differences Between Fist-Fighting and Boxing

ANGER provides the No. 1 difference between a fist-fight and a boxing bout. Anger is an unwelcome guest in any department of boxing. From the first time a chap draws on gloves as a beginner, he is taught to "keep his temper"—never to "lose his head." When a boxer gives way to anger, he becomes a "natural" fighter who tosses science into the bucket. When that occurs in the amateur or professional ring, the lost-head fighter leaves himself open and becomes an easy target for a sharpshooting opponent. Because an angry fighter usually is a helpless fighter in the ring, many prominent professionals—like Abe Attell and the late Kid McCoy—tried to taunt fiery opponents into losing their heads and "opening up." Anger rarely flares in a boxing match.

Different, indeed, is the mental condition governing a fist-fight. In that brand of combat, anger invariably is the fuel propelling one or both contestants. And when an angry, berserk chap is whaling away in a fist-fight, he usually forgets all about rules—if he ever knew any.

That brings us to difference No. 2: *the referee enforces the rules in a boxing-match; but there are no officials at a fist-fight.* Since a fist-fight has no supervision, it can develop into a roughhouse affair in which anything goes. There's no one to prevent low blows, butting, kicking, eye-gouging, biting and strangling. When angry fighters fall into a clinch, there's no one to separate them. Wrestling often ensues. A fellow may be thrown to earth, floor, or pavement. He can be hammered when down, or even be "given the boots"—

20

kicked in the face—unless some humane bystander interferes. And you can't count on bystanders.

A third difference is this: *a fist-fight is not preceded by matchmaking.* In boxing, matches are made according to weights and comparative abilities. For example, if you're an amateur or professional lightweight boxer, you'll probably be paired off against a chap of approximately your poundage—one who weighs between 133 and 137 pounds. And you'll generally be matched with a fellow whose ability is rated about on a par with your own, to insure an interesting bout and to prevent injury to either. If you boast only nine professional fights, there's little danger of your being tossed in with a top-flighter or a champion.

The eight weight divisions in boxing—heavyweight, light heavy, middle, welter, light, feather, bantam and fly—were made to prevent light men from being injured by heavy men. Weight is extremely important, you know; for moving body-weight is punch. However, when a man is a heavyweight (more than 175 pounds) there's no top limit for him or his opponent. Remember: Willard, 245; me, 180.

It's unfortunate that in fist-fighting, destiny or luck makes the matches. Chance picks your opponent for a fist-fight regardless of size, weight, age, strength or experience. Nearly every chap has had the unhappy experience of being practically forced to fight someone larger than himself at some time in his life.

A fourth difference is: *the distance or route.* Modern boxing bouts are scheduled for a specified number of rounds, with a minute of rest between. In case neither contestant is knocked out or disqualified during the bout, *The winner is determined by the number of rounds won or by the number of points scored.* When a fist-fight is started, however, it is informally slated to a " finish." There is no let-up, no rest, until one scrapper is knocked out or beaten so badly he quits. *You don't win a fist-fight on points.* Sometimes friends or the police halt a street scrap, but such interference cannot be counted upon. When a fellow squares off for a fist-fight, he should be geared to finish it. He must make his own "distance," his own "route."

Difference No. 5 is: *footing*. In the ring boxers enjoy the best footing that technicians can devise. They glide about on the firm, level surface of ring canvas. Chances of slipping are reduced to a minimum by the use of soft-leather boxing shoes; powdered resin is sprinkled on the canvas, and then the resin is ground into the soles of the shoes. Naturally there are no obstacles over which a boxer can trip, or over which he can be knocked (except, of course, the ring ropes).

The footing in fist-fights is a gamble. Fights occur usually where they flare up—on playing fields, streets, roads, ship decks, or in stores, offices, factories, saloons, dance halls, etc. And a fellow performs in whatever shoes he happens to be wearing. He fights upon whatever surface chance has placed him, regardless of slipperiness, rocks, boxes, tin cans, and the like—and regardless of tables, benches, desks, chairs or other large obstacles. If a chap slips, trips, or gets knocked over something, he may strike his head against an obstacle, or against floor, sidewalk or kerb. Many deaths have resulted from falls in fist-fights.

Let me suggest that any time you are about to be drawn into a fight, keep your head and make a split-second survey of your surroundings. Decide immediately whether you have fighting-room and whether you have good footing. If you haven't, try to force your opponent to shift to another battleground, where your knowledge of fighting will leave the percentage in your favour. Yell at him, for example: "Okay, wise guy! You want to fight! Let's see if you've got the guts to come out into the street and fight me like a man!"

In 99 out of 100 cases you can force the other guy to move to an open spot by challenging his courage to do so. Don't let the action start in a crowded subway car, in a theatre aisle, in a restaurant, office, saloon or the like. Keep your head and arrange the shift, so that you'll be able to knock his head off when you get him where you can fight without footing handicaps.

In concluding the differences, remember that your face can be cut much more quickly by a bare fist than by one encased in bandages and padded glove. From another angle, the boxer—with fist protected by bandages and glove—has less chance than the bare-fisted man of breaking a handbone or smashing a knuckle, in case the fist lands squarely on forehead or elbow.

Those major differences add up to one important total or conclusion: *the possibility of getting hurt is greater in a fistfight than in a boxing bout. Fist-fighting is generally more dangerous than boxing.* In connection with that danger, never forget: the longer the fight lasts, the longer you are exposed to danger. Moreover, the danger percentage against you generally increases with each passing minute of the fight. When you square off, you hope to beat your opponent into submission in a hurry. But, as the fist-fight continues, you find you are not achieving your quick victory. You discover you are beginning to tire because of your exertions and because of your tensions. Since you have no chance for rest periods, the longer you fight the more tired you become.

True, your opponent also may be getting fatigued; but you can't be certain about his exact condition unless he's blowing and staggering. You know for sure only that you're nearly "all in," and that he's still out there swinging at you. Accordingly, the longer he keeps fighting, the less chance you have of winning; but the greater chance you have of being battered, cut up, knocked down, knocked out, or injured. Because of the danger in a fist-fight, it is imperative that you end the brawl as quickly as possible; and the best way to do that is by a knockout. The knockout is far more important in fist-fighting than in boxing. *You've got to knock 'em out in fist-fights.*

Chapter 6: You're the Kayo Kid

To PROTECT yourself with your fists, you *must* become a knockout puncher. And you may do that within three months, if you're a normal chap—anywhere between twelve and thirty. By "normal" I mean healthy and sound—neither ailing nor crippled.

You should be able to knock out a fellow of approximately your own weight, with either fist, if you follow my instructions exactly and practice them diligently. And in six months or a year, you may be able to knock out fellows a lot bigger and heavier than you are. You've got the weight and the machinery. In fact, you're the Kayo Kid.

And just as soon as you savvy the knockout punch, I'll take you along through the other departments of fighting. When you finish these instructions, you'll know exactly how to be a well-rounded scrapper. You'll be able to use your fists so destructively and practically that, with experience, you'll be able to move into amateur or even professional competition if you so desire. Should you go into competition, you'll have a big advantage in all-round fighting knowledge over most boys who came up during the past quarter-century.

Remember this: You don't have to be an athlete to learn how to use your fists. And it doesn't matter whether you're tall or short, fat or skinny, timid or brave. Regardless of your size, shape or courage, you already have the weapons with which to protect yourself. I repeat: All you have to do is learn to use them correctly.

It's true that nearly every guy can fight a little bit *naturally*, without having anyone show him the right way. It's true also that the average boy or man might sit down at a piano and be able to pick out some sort of tune with one finger; or he might use the "hunt and peck" system on a typewriter until he had written a couple of lines; or he might jump into a pool and swim a bit with the dog-paddle or with his version of the breast stroke. But he never could become a good pianist without being taught to play correctly. He never could become a fast, accurate typist without being drilled in the touch system. And he never could become a speed swimmer without being shown the crawl stroke.

It's no more natural for a beginner to step out and fight correctly than for a novice to step out and skate correctly or dive correctly or dance the tango or do the slalom on skis. Even Babe Ruth and Joe Louis, despite their prowess in other fields, were beginners when they took up golf; and each had to learn to swing a golf club correctly in order to assure accuracy and distance in his drive.

It's strange but true that *certain fundamental movements seem unnatural* to the beginner in nearly every activity *requiring close co-ordination between body and mind*. Fist-fighting is no exception. Some of the fundamental moves seem awkwardly unnatural when first tried. That's particularly true of the movements in explosive long-range straight punching, the basic weapon in fist-fighting or boxing.

In fighting, as in many other activities, it's *natural* for the beginner to do the *wrong* thing. It's natural for him to *swing* rather than punch *straight*. It's natural for him to hit with the *wrong* knuckles of his fist. It's natural for him to use leg-tangling footwork, etc. Let me emphasize again that you will feel very awkward when you first try the moves in long-range punching. I stress that awkwardness for two reasons: (1) so that you won't figure you're a hopeless palooka, and (2) so that you'll pay no attention to wisecracks of friends or sideline experts who watch your early flounderings. Remember: He laughs last who hits hardest.

Chapter 7: What Is a Punch?

NATURE has given you, a normal beginner, the three requisites for a knockout punch. They are:

1. *Weight—the weight of your entire body.*
2. *Powerful muscles in your feet, legs and back—the means of helping to* PUT YOUR BODYWEIGHT INTO MOTION.
3. *Arms and fists—the means of* EXPLODING *your moving weight against an opponent.*

For practical purposes, I divide a punch into two parts: (a) setting the weight in motion, and (b) relaying the moving weight to a desired point on an opponent with a stepped-up impact or explosion.

All full-fledged punches must have that (a) and (b) combination. It is only in what might be called "partial" punches that the body-weight does not play a stellar role. Partial punches are those delivered with only the weight of arms and fists—short backhands to the head, chops to the kidney or to the back of the neck, or mere cuffs to the head when in a tight clinch.

Since we're concerned primarily with the stunning, full-fledged knockout punch, let's move on to it. Let's examine the first fundamental. How do we set the body-weight in motion?

There are four ways of setting the body-weight in motion for punching: (1) falling forward; (2) springing forward; (3) whirling the shoulders by means of the powerful back muscles, assisted by shifting weight from one leg to the other, and (4) by surging upwards, as in delivering uppercuts. Every punch combines at least two of those motion-methods.

Best of all the punches is the "stepping straight jolt,"

delivered with either fist from the "falling step." It has fall, spring and whirl. That stepping jolt must not be confused with the "ordinary straight punch" that is delivered at medium range without moving the feet, and that depends almost entirely on shoulder whirl. The stepping jolt is a much more explosive blow.

Hooks and uppercuts are short-range blows that can be just as explosive as stepping jolts. However, the hooks and

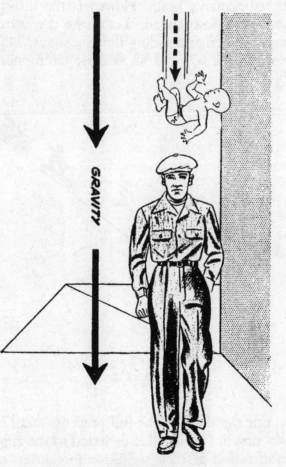

FIGURE 1

uppercuts are less desirable for fist-fighting, in which one tries to keep at long range as much as possible in order to avoid clinching and wrestling.

How does a fighter set his weight in motion *by a fall?*

The falling procedure is simple. Remember the baby and the truck driver? The baby fell straight down from the fourth-floor window (Figure 1). It was yanked straight toward the earth by gravity. It encountered nothing to change the direction of its moving body-weight until it struck the truckman's head. However, the direction of a falling object can be changed. Let's take the example of a boy sitting on a sled and sliding down a snowy hill (Figure 2). In a sense, the boy and his sled are falling objects, like

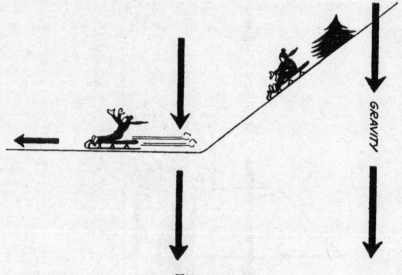

FIGURE 2

the baby. But the slope of the hill prevents them from falling straight down. Their fall is deflected to the angle of the hill. The direction of their weight-in-motion is on a slant. And when they reach the level plain at the bottom of the hill, they will continue to slide for a while. However, the direction of their slide on the plain—the direction of their weight-in-motion—will be *straight out,* at a right angle to the straight-down pull of gravity.

Those examples of the falling baby and the sledding boy illustrate two basic principles of the stepping jolt: (1) that gravity can give motion to weight by causing a *fall,* and (2) the direction of that weight-in-motion can be deflected away from the perpendicular—on a slant, or straight forward. "But," you ask, "what's the connection between all that falling stuff and the straight jolt?"

I'll answer that question by letting you take your first step as a puncher, and I do mean s-t-e-p.

Chapter 8: The Falling Step

Stand in the middle of the floor. Point your *left* foot at any distant object in the room. Place your *right* foot to the rear and slightly to the right of your *left* foot (Figure 3). For a chap about five feet 10 inches tall, the heel of his *right* foot should be about 18 inches back (and slightly to the right) of the heel of his *left* foot.

Let your arms dangle loosely at your sides; you won't need to use them in the step.

Bend your knees slightly. Bend your body forward slightly as you shift your *weight forward on to your left foot,* so that your *right foot* is resting only lightly on the ball of the foot. Remember that the knees are still slightly bent. Teeter up and down easily (half-bouncing without leaving the floor) to make certain you're in a comfortable, balanced position. If your position does not feel balanced and comfortable, move your right foot about slightly—but not much—to get a better balance as you teeter. You are resting only lightly on the ball of your *right* foot, remember. Stop teetering, but keep the knees slightly bent and your arms at your side.

Now—*without any preliminary movement*—take a *long,* quick step forward with your *left* foot, toward the object at which your *left* toe had been pointing (Figure 4). I emphasize: *no preliminary movement before the step.* You unquestionably will be tempted to shift some of the weight from the *left* foot to the *right* foot just before you step. But don't do it. Do nothing with the *right* foot, which is resting lightly on its ball. *No preliminary movement!* Just lift the *left* foot and *let the body fall forward in a long, quick step.*

FIGURE 3   FIGURE 4

The *left* foot should land flat and solid on the floor at the end of the step.

It is a quick, convulsive and extremely awkward step. Yet, it's one of the most important steps of your fistic life; for that falling-forward lurch is the rough diamond out of which will be ground the beautiful, straight knockout jolt. It's the gem-movement of straight punching. Try that falling step many times. Make certain, each time, that you start

31

from a comfortably balanced position, that the body-weight is resting largely on the *left* leg, that the knees are slightly bent, that the arms are at your side, and that you make no preliminary movement with the *right* foot.

I call that forward lurch a "falling step." Actually, every step in walking involves a small "fall." Walking is a series of "falls." But in this particular step, the fall is exaggerated for two reasons: (1) your weight is well forward when you step off, and (2) the step is so long that it gives gravity a chance to impart unusual momentum to your body-weight. The solidity with which your *left* foot landed upon the floor was caused by your momentum. The late Joe Gans rarely missed with a long, straight punch; but, when he did you could hear for half a block the smack of his left sole on the canvas.

Although the weight of your body was resting largely upon your *left* foot when you stepped off, you didn't fall to the floor. Why? Because the alert ball of your *right* foot came to the rescue frantically and gave your body a forward *spring* in a desperate attempt to keep your body balanced upright—to maintain its equilibrium. Your rescuing *right foot* acted not only as did the slope of the hill for the sledding boy, but also as a *springboard* in the side of the hill might have functioned had the sledding boy whizzed onto a spring-board on the side of the hill. The *left foot* serves as a "trigger" to spring the *right foot*. So, the falling step sometimes is called the Trigger Step.

I warned: *don't make a preliminary movement* before stepping off. Had you followed your natural inclination and shifted your weight to the right foot before stepping, that action would have started your body-weight *moving backward*—away from the direction in which you intended to step. Then you would have had to lose a split-second while your *right* foot was stopping the backward motion and shifting your weight forward again before the punching step could be taken.

Learn now and remember always that in fighting you cannot afford to give your body the luxury of a useless preliminary or preparatory movement before shooting a punch. In the first place, your target may be open for only a split-second, and you must take advantage of that opening like a bolt of lightning. Secondly, preliminary movements are give-aways—"tell-tales"—"telegraphs"—that treacherously betray to your opponent your own next action. Joe Louis was knocked out in his first fight with Max Schmeling principally because tell-tale movements of Joe's left glove disclosed the fact that he was preparing to shoot a left jab. Schmeling timed Joe's telegraphs and smashed him again and again with straight rights to the head. Herr Maxie smashed him every time that careless left hand beckoned.

You now know how to set your weight into motion for a straight jolt—by means of the *falling step*. Next we must consider the second part of the jolt: *conveying the moving body-weight and exploding it against your opponent*.

However, before studying the *movements* in conveyance and explosion, it will be necessary for you to understand clearly the *line of power* that all successful conveyance and explosion must follow.

Chapter 9: The Power Line

THE movements in the second part of a straight jolt are just as simple as those in the " falling step "; yet, strangely enough, that part of the punch has been the big blind spot in hitting since the days of Jim Figg in the early 1700's. He was the father of modern boxing. By the time John L. Sullivan and later "old masters" came along, many outstanding punchers had eliminated that blind spot with their knowledge of punching technique. But today that area of darkness is bigger than at any time since Corbett beat Sullivan.

At least nine of every ten fellows who try to box never become good punchers because they never learn how to make their arms and fists *serve efficiently* as conveyors and exploders. They become " powder-puff " punchers or, at best, only fair hitters. Their punches lack *body-weight*, *explosion* and *follow-through*. Such failure can be prevented by *power-line punching*.

What is the *power line? The power line runs from either shoulder—straight down the length of the arm—to the* FIST KNUCKLE OF THE LITTLE FINGER, when the fist is doubled. Remember: The power line ends in the first knuckle of the little finger on either hand. Gaze upon your " pinky " with new respect. You might call that pinky knuckle the *exit of your power line*—the muzzle of your cannon. You'll understand the power line if you feel it out.

Stand up. Walk toward a wall until you're at arm's length from the wall when facing it. Put your heels together. You should be standing just far enough from the wall so that you can barely touch it with the tip of the *middle* finger of your *right* hand—at a *point directly opposite your chin*. Touch that chin-high point with your middle-finger tip. Now, move back three or four inches, but keep the heels together. Double your *right fist* firmly. In *making a fist*, close the fingers into the palm of the hand, and then close the thumb down over the outside of the fingers (Figure 5).

FIGURE 5

Extend the fist at arm's length *toward* the spot on the wall —only toward it. The fist should be *upright*, as if you were holding a stick running from ceiling to floor. The little knuckle is down, toward the floor. With your arm *stiffly extended*, let your body sway slowly forward—without moving the feet—until your fist (still upright) is pressed so firmly against the chin-high spot on the wall that your fist and stiff arm are *supporting the weight of your leaning body* (Figure 6).

35

FIGURE 6

Note that the lower part of your fist (still upright)—
particularly the *little knuckle*—provides the natural, *solid*
end of the firm, straight line—from shoulder to fist—that is
supporting your weight. Note particularly that this line runs
unswervingly *through your wrist* to the little knuckle
(Figure 7). Now, with your upright fist still supporting
your weight at the chin-high spot, try to shift your pressure
from the little knuckle *to the upper knuckles*. Then turn
your fist so that the palm of your hand is down. When you

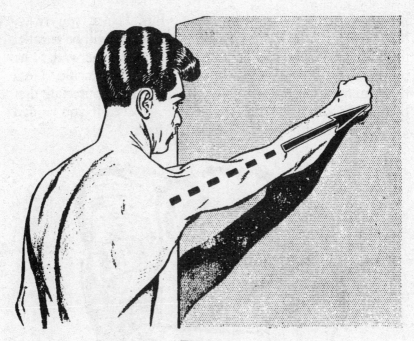

FIGURE 7

attempt those changes, you should feel immediately that both new pressure positions of your fist lack the solidity of the first position. And you should feel and see that a change in position *swerved* the power line at the wrist—putting your wrist in a hazardous landing position.

Keeping your feet in the same position, go through *the same procedure with your left fist.* You'll find the power line in the same location—straight from shoulder through the little knuckle. But, where would the power line be if you wished to lower your fists and punch at a man's stomach?

You can answer that by testing a spot on the wall just oposite your own solar plexus—the vital body target just below the end of the breast bone. In making the lower test, sway forward from the same standing position—with either

37

fist—toward the solar-plexus spot. But, before you sway, *turn your fist palm-down* so that the knuckles will be parallel to the ceiling when you press your fist against the wall. The power line still runs solidly through the little knuckle. Now that you have felt out the power line, you can appreciate that the greatest possible solidity would be achieved if you landed every punch with the little knuckle first.

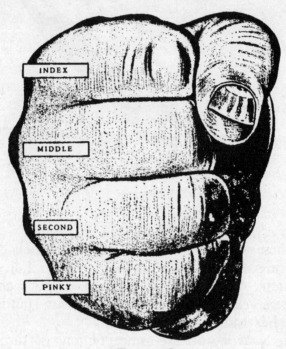

FIGURE 8

Unfortunately, however, the hand-bone behind the little knuckle is the most fragile of the five back-bones. It can be broken most easily. *You must not attempt to land first with the little knuckle.* Instead you must TRY TO LAND FIRST WITH THE KNUCKLE NEXT TO YOUR PINKY (Figure 8). We'll call that the *second knuckle.* Aiming with the second knuckle usually brings about a *three-knuckle* landing. Those three *landing knuckles are middle, second* and *pinky*. If you aim with the second knuckle, those three knuckles usually will land together because the average fist *slopes slightly from the middle knuckle to the pinky*. Such a three-knuckle landing not only prevents the hand-bone behind any one knuckle from bearing all the punch-shock, but it also permits punching *almost exactly along the power line*. Rarely will one of those knuckles make a solo landing. But if you aim with the little knuckle, you risk a dangerous solo landing on forehead on blocking elbow.

Always aim with the second knuckle—the one next to your pinky—and *let the other knuckles take care of themselves*. They'll take care of themselves all right; for the shape of the fist makes it impossible for them to do otherwise. Clench your right fist and inspect its knuckles. Your *thumb* knuckle is "out of the way"—completely separated from your row of four knuckles on the striking edge of your fist. More than that, your thumb knuckle is farthest away from your pinky knuckle—farthest away from the end of the power line. Nature took care of that. Never double-cross nature by trying to hit with that thumb knuckle, *under any circumstance*. It breaks easily. Keep it out of the way.

The knuckle of your *index finger* (the one next to the thumb) is fairly prominent, but not as prominent as the knuckle of your *middle finger*. In some face-punches and in most body-blows, that *index knuckle* will land with the other three, for a four-knuckle landing. That's okay, let the index knuckle *come along for the ride*. Under no circumstances, however, try to land first with that index knuckle. If you do, you'll not only break your *power line*, but you may also break your wrist.

Beware likewise of trying to land first with the prominent middle knuckle—the source of most hand injuries. Such aiming will slant your hand off the power line and, at the same time, endanger the middle knuckle and its hand-bone. When that middle knuckle makes a solo landing, its

39

prominence prevents the other knuckles from helping to absorb some of the punch-shock. That shock or pressure is terrific in any full-fledged punch, particularly when you nail an opponent with a head blow *just as he is stepping into you*. In that split-second, your fist must withstand the shock pressure of an explosive collision between two hurtling body-weights.

Let me repeat: If your punch is landed correctly, in power-line fashion, the three knuckles—pinky, second and middle—will share the pressure and distribute it over the three hand-bones behind the knuckles. That lessens the chance of bruising or crushing any one knuckle, or of fracturing any one hand-bone. Most professional and amateur boxers suffer hand injuries during their careers even though their fists are protected by bandages, tape and gloves, because they don't make a fist properly. As I pointed out earlier, the hands HAVE NO SUCH PROTECTION IN A FIST-FIGHT. You must land correctly, not only for power-line explosiveness, but for hand protection.

We have examined the power line and second-knuckle aiming for long-range straight jolts; but what about other types of punches? What about medium-range straight punches, and hooks and uppercuts? Does the power line and the second-knuckle aim hold good for them?

Yes, indeed, they do hold good. *You must hit along the power line in* ALL *full-fledged punches*; AND YOU MUST ALWAYS AIM WITH THE SECOND KNUCKLE.

The landing position of your fist may change from upright to sideways, in varying degrees, when shooting different types of punches for the head. And it may change in various degrees from sideways to upright in punching for the body. *But always you must punch along the power line, and always you must aim with the second knuckle.* You'll get the feel of that power line in other punches later. You'll discover that bending the elbow, in a hook, for example, does not break the line of power. And you'll find out why.

Chapter 10: Relaying and Exploding

You have learned how to set your body-weight into motion for a long-range jolt. And you have located the power line and its exit. Now you are ready to learn the "relay and explosion." You can do that best by throwing a jolt.

First, we must get something to punch—something you can hit solidly without injuring your fists. If you can go into a gymnasium, swell; for in a gym you'll find an inflated, pear-shaped, light, leather striking bag (Figure 9), and a large, heavy, cylindrical canvas or leather "dummy bag" —sometimes known as the "heavy bag" (Figure 10). The latter is packed with cotton waste, but it is solid enough for you to accustom your fists, wrists and arms to withstand considerable punching shock. One can practise both body and head blows on the heavy bag. On the fast light bag—which is about the height of an opponent's head—one can sharpen one's speed and timing for "head-hunting"; and one also can practise the important back-hand, warding-off stroke until it becomes automatic.

If no gymnasium is available, and if you are unable to buy bags from an athletic-goods store, you'll have to carry on without a light bag and make your own heavy bag. To make the dummy bag, get two empty gunny sacks. Put one sack inside the other to give your bag double strength. Then fill the inside sack with old rags, excelsior, old furniture-filling, or the like. Sawdust mixed with the above makes an excellent filler. *Make certain there are no solid objects in the stuffing of your bag.* Leave enough space at the top so that you can wrap the necks of both bags securely with a rope. Suspend the bag on the rope from a strong girder in

FIGURE 9

your basement, barn or woodshed—or even from the limb of a tree. Do not attempt to use the heavy bag in your living quarters; the pounding vibrations will loosen the plaster in walls and ceiling.

Whether you practise punching in a gymnasium or at home, you must use *striking gloves* (not boxing gloves) to protect the skin on your knuckles (Figure 11). If you can't buy the small, mittenlike leather striking gloves, make a pair

FIGURE 10

of your own by snipping the fingers off a pair of *leather work* gloves, midway down each finger. Cutting them off in this fashion will permit you to clench your fists freely. Even with the protection of striking gloves, you'll probably skin your knuckles during the first three weeks of punching practice. However, the knuckles will become calloused gradually.

Now that you have some sort of heavy bag and some sort of striking gloves, you are ready to begin throwing punches.

43

FIGURE 11

You're ready to *step*, *relay* and *explode*. Do it as follows:

Put on your striking gloves. Take your falling-step position before the bag. The toe of your left foot should be pointing straight at the bag, and the toe-tip should be about three feet out from the bag. Practise the falling step three or four times, with your arms at your sides.

Now, again take your position for the falling step. As you teeter up and down, raise your relaxed arms into guarding position (Figure 12). As you raise them, also raise your *left* shoulder slightly and shove the *left* shoulder forward a trifle, so that your chin—snuggling beside it—would be protected from a blow coming at any angle from your own left. *Keep your elbows in*, toward your body. Your relaxed hands are *half-opened*, with thumbs resting easily upon the

FIGURE 12

index fingers. The upper knuckle of your *left thumb* should be about ten inches forward from your lips. The upper knuckle of your *right thumb* should be about four inches forward from your lips.

Teeter in that position until you feel balanced and comfortable. *Be relaxed everywhere as you teeter.* If you feel cramped by holding your elbows in, let them out slightly, but only slightly.

FIGURE 13A

Now—when you feel comfortable and relaxed—*suddenly do the falling step toward the bag* (Figure 13), and as you step, *make the following moves*:

1. Shoot your loose, half-opened *left hand* straight along the power line at a chin-high spot on the bag.

2. But, as the relaxed *left* hand speeds toward the bag, *suddenly close the hand with a convulsive, grabbing snap.* Close it with such a terrific grab that when the second

46

knuckle of the upright fist smashes into the bag, the *fist and the arm and the shoulder will be " frozen " steel-hard by the terrific grabbing tension.*

That convulsive, freezing grab is the *explosion*.

Try that long left jolt three or four times. Make certain each time that (1) you are completely relaxed before you step; (2) that your relaxed LEFT hand, in normal guarding position, is only half-closed; (3) that you make no pre-

47

liminary movement with either your feet or your left hand. Do not draw back—or "cock"—the relaxed left hand in a preparatory movement that you hope will give the punch more zing. *Don't do that!* You'll not only telegraph the blow, but you'll slow up and weaken the punch.

Now that you've got the *feel* of the stepping jolt, let's examine it in slow motion to see exactly what you did.

First, the Falling Step launched your body-weight straight at the target at which your left toe was pointing.

Secondly, your relaxed left hand shot out to relay that moving body-weight along the power line to the target *before that moving weight could be relayed to the floor by your descending left foot.*

Thirdly, the convulsive, desperate grab in your explosion accomplished the following: (a) caused the powerful muscles of your back to give your left shoulder a slight surging whirl toward your own right, (b) psychologically "pulled" the moving body-weight into your arm with a sudden lurch, (c) gave a lightning boost to the speed of your fist, (d) froze your fist, wrist, arm and shoulder along the power line at the instant your fist smashed into the target, and (e) caused terrific "*follow-through*" after the explosion.

When the long, straight jolt crashes into a fellow's chin, the fist doesn't bounce off harmlessly, as it might in a light, medium-range left jab. No sir! The frozen solidity behind the jolt causes the explosion to shoot forward as the solid breech of a rifle forces a cartridge explosion to shoot the bullet forward. The bullet in a punch is your fist, with the combined power from your fast-moving weight and your convulsing muscles behind it—solidly. Your fist, exploded forward by the solid power behind it, has such terrific "follow-through" that it can snap back an opponent's head like that of a shot duck. It can smash his nose, knock out his teeth, break his jaw, stun him, floor him, knock him out.

What was your right hand doing while your left delivered its first power punch?

Your *right* hand should have been in a position of alertness to protect you from a countering blow or to follow with another punch to your opponent's chin. As your *left hand* sped towards its target; your *right hand*, rising slightly from its original guarding position, should have opened—with all fingers, including the thumb, pressing tightly against each other to form a "knife blade"—and should have turned its palm slightly toward the bag, as if you were about to chop an opponent's *left* shoulder with the outer edge of your *right hand*. However, you do no chopping; instead, your *right hand* merely remains tensely alert until the *left fist* lands.

Try a few more *left* jolts. Make certain each time that your *right hand* becomes an alert "knife." (See Figure 13.) Perhaps you wondered why I started you punching with the *left hand* instead of with the *right* inasmuch as we are seeking speedy development of a knockout blow. I started you with the *left* for several reasons.

Contrary though it may seem, the *left* fist is more important for a *right-handed* fighter (not a southpaw) than is the *right fist*. That is true because, in normal punching position, the *left* hand is closer than the *right* to an opponent's head or body. Since it is closer, the *left* is harder for any opponent to avoid than the more distant *right*. If you can land solidly with a straight left or with a left hook, you'll generally knock your opponent off balance, at least, and "set him up" for a pot-shot with your right.

It's not only easier to hit an opponent with your *left*, but it's also *safer*. When you shoot the left, your chin is protected partially by your left shoulder and partially by your guarding right hand. Because it is easier and safer to use the left, you usually *lead* with that fist. When two fighters are warily watching each other, waiting for an opening at any time during an encounter, the first punch thrown (by either)

49

is a *lead*. It's so dangerous to lead with the right against an experienced opponent that the *right lead* is called a *sucker punch*. However, there are times when the *right lead* can be used with deadly effectiveness, as Schmeling demonstrated in his first fight with Louis.

In addition, use of the falling step practically guarantees your developing a solid left jolt. You have no such assurance, if you try to develop a good straight left from the medium-range shoulder whirl—the method by which most current fighters put their body-weight into motion for all straight punches. I'll explain later why straight punches that are powered only by shoulder whirl cannot have effective follow-through. Right now let me merely point out that when a fellow stands in normal punching position, with weight forward and with his left shoulder slightly forward to protect his chin, he can get very little shoulder whirl into a left jolt —unless he draws back his left shoulder. Such a move would be a cardinal sin.

I use the expression " left jolt " instead of " left jab " because I don't want you to confuse the type of straight left you will throw, with the futile straight left or " jab " used by most current amateur and professional boxers. Most of them couldn't knock your hat off with their left jabs. With their lefts, they tap, they slap, they flick, they paw, they " paint." Their jabs are used more to confuse than to stun. Their jabs are used as shuttering defensive flags to prevent their poorly instructed opponents from " getting set to punch." A good fighter doesn't have to " get set." He's always ready to punch. Some of them use their jabs merely to make openings for their rights. And that's dangerously silly, for the proper brand of feinting would accomplish the same purpose. With but few exceptions, they *do not use the left jab as a smashing jolt that can be an explosive weapon by itself*—that can knock you down or knock you out.

There are two reasons why the left jolt is a rarity in fighting today. First, nearly all current boxers launch their jabs with the non-step shoulder whirl. Secondly, nearly all have been fed the defensive hokum that it's less dangerous to try to tap an opponent with the left than to try to knock him down with the left.

Concerning that defensive hokum, let me say this: Any time you extend your left fist either for a tap or for an all-out punch, you're taking a gamble on being nailed with a counter-punch. And the sap who uses "light stuff"—tapping, flicking, etc.—has his left hand extended much more often than the explosive left-jolter, who doesn't waste punches—doesn't shoot until he has feinted or forced his opponent into an opening. It's true that you can "recover" your balance more quickly after missing a tap than after missing a hard punch. But it's also true that an opponent who is defending only against taps and slaps will be much more alert to counter than will an opponent who is being *bombed*.

My advice to all beginners is this: Use a light left jab only in one instance—in the so-called one-two punch—when your left fist strikes the opponent's forehead to tip his head back, so that your immediately following straight right can nail him on the chin. Speaking of straight rights, I'll let you throw one now. *The straight right jolt is thrown from the same position as the straight left.* Stand in your normal punching position. Your relaxed *right hand* is half-opened, and the upper knuckle of the thumb is about four inches in front of your lips.

Without any preliminary movement of the right hand, shoot it at the chin-high spot on the bag as you do the falling step. Neither pull back nor cock the right before throwing it. As you step in to explode the second knuckle of your upright fist against the bag, your chin should be partially protected by your *left* shoulder, *left* arm and *left* hand. Remember that you *left* hand opens to make a "knife blade," with the palm turned slightly toward your opponent. While the *right* fist is being thrown, the *left* hand and arm

51

should stiffen for an instant in order to present a rigid barrier before the face in case an opponent attempts to strike with a countering right. The *index knuckle* of your opened *left hand* should remain about ten inches in front of your left eye as you step in. But the instant your *right* fist lands, your *left* hand should relax into its normal half-opened condition so that it will be ready to punch immediately, if necessary.

Straight punches for the body, with either hand, are begun and executed in the same manner as head punches. (Any change in position before the start would be a tell-tale.) When in motion, however, your fist turns so that the palm is down when the second knuckle explodes against the bag. Also, *as you begin* the body punch, you bend forward to slide under guarding arms and to make your own chin a less open target.

As you practise those punches, *keep your eyes wide open*. Don't close your eyes as you step in. Focus your eyes on your target. *You must keep your eyes wide open at all times when you are fighting or boxing.*

Keep your eyes open; but *keep your ears closed* to the kibitzers and wise guys who may scoff at your early awkwardness in using the *trigger step*. They may tell you that you're charging like a war horse. They may tell you that you're merely poking as you would with a stick. They may tell you that *every straight punch to the head should land with the fist in a palm-down position*. They may tell you that you are completely off balance and that you must have a slow recovery if you miss with a stepping punch.

You are *not* charging; you are being *shot* forward. You are not *poking*; you are *exploding*. A stepping straight punch to the head should land with the fist in an *upright* position to keep the punch *straight*. The instant you turn your fist to land palm-down in a head punch, you will begin to loop the punch. You'll learn all about looping later, when you study straight punches that are delivered from the shoulder whirl, without the step. Don't concern yourself now with balance and recovery. You are punching from the proper *stance*. As your feet, legs, and arms accustom themselves to the falling, power-line explosions, they will take care of your balance and recovery. They'll make certain that you are still in normal punching stance, whether you land on your target or whether you miss.

Don't let anyone induce you to shorten your step before you have mastered this type of punching. You must become an expert in using the comparatively long step for two reasons: (1) in no other way can you become an *explosive* long-range *sharpshooter*, particularly with your left hand; and (2) in no other way can you so accustom your body to the lightning forward lurch that the movement becomes instinctive. Later, when the trigger step has become a habit, your body will bolt forward—whether you step two feet or two inches.

To make your early practice sessions with the basic, long-range blows more interesting, I'll tell you now about stance, and then teach you the fundamentals of footwork.

Chapter 11 : Stance

STANCE *is the customary posture or position out of which a fighter operates.*

There are three principal types of stance (Figure 14):

1. *The upright stance.* In that position, used by many British boxers, the body is practically *straight up and down*, with the weight either evenly distributed on both feet or resting largely upon the *right* foot. It is an excellent *defensive* stance because it permits freedom of the feet for fast footwork, and because it provides freedom for blocking and parrying. It has at least one *defensive weakness*, however. The user can be knocked off balance or floored much more easily than if the weight is forward. *Offensively*, the position does *not stimulate explosive punching*, since the weight is not forward.

2. *The semi-crouch.* That's the stance you've been using for throwing straight explosive punches. I'll explain shortly why it's the *perfect stance for fist-fighting*.

3. *The full crouch*, or low crouch. That stance is used at close quarters by practically all "bobbers and weavers"— chaps who come in bobbing low and weaving from side to side. It is used by those who specialize in hooking attacks rather than in straight punching. The bobber-weaver prefers to fight at close quarters, for all hooks and uppercuts are most explosive at short range. It is an *excellent defensive stance* after the user has mastered the art of bobbing and weaving. That takes considerable time. Your bobbing-weaving head is an elusive target. Moreover, you are bent forward so far that your opponent has great difficulty getting at your body. It was my favourite stance. I found it

invaluable in fighting bigger men. It has these disadvantages. Your weight is too far forward to permit proper "fall" in straight stepping jolts. And your weight is too far forward to permit fast retreating footwork—if you want to retreat.

If a fellow is a *southpaw*—left-handed—he can use any of the three stances; but his *right* foot and *right* hand will be *forward* and the *left* foot and *left* hand to the *rear*. It is

55

FIGURE 14C

much easier for a left-handed chap to fight in southpaw style. However, most trainers prefer to convert southpaws —to turn them round—and have them take a right-handed stance.

The *semi-crouch*, which you have been using, is *the best stance for fist-fighting* for the following reasons: (a) Your weight is forward just enough to stimulate explosive straight punching; (b) it is forward enough to prevent you being knocked off balance or floored easily; (c) nevertheless, the weight is not forward so far as to interfere with your footwork—and footwork is important in keeping you at long range in a fist-fight; (d) you are at all times in a comfortably balanced position from which you can attack, counter, or defend—*without preliminary movement.*

Chapter 12: Footwork

Take your punching stance, *about 10 feet from the bag*. Teeter for balance and relaxation. Now, take a short shuffling step forward with your *left foot*—a step of about 8 inches (Figure 15). Let your *right foot* follow automatically and assume its normal position, your weight resting lightly upon the ball of the foot. Continue shuffling toward the bag in that fashion. Try to refrain from rocking back and forth like a hobby-horse as you advance. Instead, make your progress a comparatively smooth glide, with your knees slightly bent *and with your body always in punching position.*

When you reach striking range of the bag, step in with a straight jolt with either fist—*without preliminary movement*. I mean: *your last shuffling step takes you within range, and your next step is the punching step.* Under no circumstances take any little half-step or hippity-hop when you decide to punch. *And don't draw back the punching hand.* Practise the shuffling approach a few times, hitting with one fist and then the other.

Next, try the *shuffle backward* (See Figure 15A, lower panel). Take your punching position within striking range of the bag. Instead of stepping into the bag with a punch, slide your *right foot* back about 8 inches from its original position. Let your left foot follow back automatically until it's in normal distance of your right. Remember that your weight has been kept well forward as you (1) slid your right foot back, and (2) let the left foot follow it. Continue shuffling backward away from the bag until you've taken 10 or 12 steps.

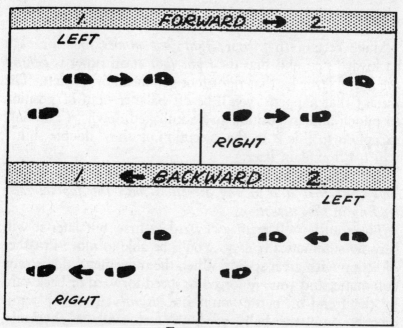

FIGURE 15A

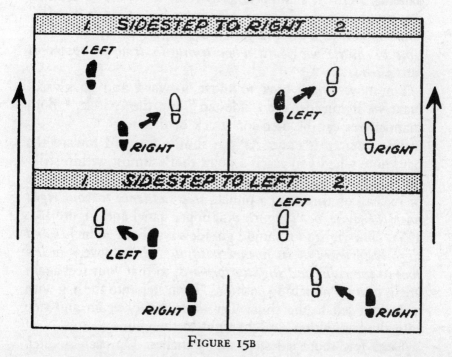

FIGURE 15B

59

Make certain that your *right foot moves first* for each backward step and that the *right foot* at all times is *behind the left*. Never let that right foot get ahead of the left. The instant that happens, you'll be off balance—out of position to punch and in position to be knocked down. (The only exception to this is in the execution of the "double shift," which I'll explain later.)

Remember this fundamental of footwork: *you always make the first step in any direction with the foot already leading in that direction.*

The shuffle will seem awkward at first, but later it will become automatically easy. You'll be able to move in either direction with great speed. When the movements do become automatic, and you are forced to speed forward or backward by the trend of battle you'll rise *slightly* from the semi-crouch—onto the balls of both feet—with a rhythmic, dancing step. It's important to remember, however, that *you do not use the dancing step if you have time to "stalk" your opponent with the forward shuffle; or, if you have time to shuffle backward when trying to draw an opponent into a lead.*

You now know how to move forward and backward. Next we'll consider the "sidestep" and the "circle." Both manoeuvres can be used for attack or defence.

The *sidestep* is easy. As you shuffle forward toward the bag, note when you reach a point that's almost within striking range. Then, instead of taking another forward step or instead of throwing a punch, *step suddenly to your right with the right foot* (Figure 15B, upper panel and Figure 16A, 16B). The right foot should go sideways about 20 inches *and slightly forward of its former position.* Then move your *left foot to the right and slightly forward*, so that your feet again are in normal punching position. Then step into the bag with a straight left to the chin. Try those moves again and step into the bag with a straight right to the chin.

Do a few more sidesteps and punches. On each sidestep

FIGURE 16A   FIGURE 16B

to the right, make certain that *your right foot is moving first.*
Do not try to punch while taking the sidestep. Punch after
your lightning sidestep has been completed. Your quick
sidestep will force your opponent to break from his normal
position just as he was "getting set" probably to punch at
you or to defend. Your sidestep should prevent his
immediate punching and, at the same time, cause him
perhaps to leave an opening for your lead.

CIRCLE the bag to your right by *making a series of side-steps to the right*, without pausing to punch. Make certain, however, that at the completion of each sidestep in the circle *you are facing the bag in normal punching position*. Make certain also that *your left leg never crosses the right*.

Next, circle—with three or four sidesteps—and then step into the bag with a left jolt. Then, circle and step in with a right. *Sidestepping and circling to the left* are done in practically the same way as moving to the right, except that *your left foot always takes the first step to the left* (See Figure 15B, lower panel).

Be certain that your hands and arms are in their normal defensive positions as you circle, and particularly when you move to your own *left*, which is toward your opponent's right. *For purely defensive purposes*, both the sidestep and the circle are extremely useful against an opponent who rushes you.

If you practise footwork and long-range punching at a bag, you'll soon be able to knock out the average chap of approximately your own weight in a fist-fight. You'll be able to do that, even if you never learn anything more about fighting, or even if you have no chance to practise your punches against a " live target "—another fellow. You'll have explosives *in your hands*, and it's a hundred-to-one bet that Mr. Average Chap will not. *But you should learn more*—much more—to make you a well-rounded scrapper. You should learn the various types of punches from the whirl and from the surge, and the fundamentals of *aggressive defence*.

Chapter 13: Range

You should understand and appreciate "range" before you learn punching from the whirl or from the surge.

When you're in a normal punching position, *range is the distance between your right fist and your No. 1 target: your opponent's chin.* The *right fist* determines the *range*; for if you haven't punching room for the *right*, you *certainly* won't have punching room for the more forward *left*.

There are three general classifications of "range" (Figure 17A, B, C):

1. *Long range.* That's the range for explosive sharp-shooting. It's the range at which most leading is done. At that range you're far enough from your opponent so that you can *step in* with a full-fledged straight punch. It can be either a lead or a counter-punch. You've already learned that the falling step is used for launching your weight in long-range hitting.

2. *Medium range.* That's the range for rapid-fire straight-punching exchanges. You are rarely at medium range when not exchanging. At that range you have room to throw straight punches, but you lack the room to step. For those straight punches your weight is given motion principally by the shoulder whirl instead of by the falling step. If you're lucky, you may be able to develop a knockout straight punch from the shoulder whirl. *But you'll never be able to develop from the shoulder whirl a straight punch that's as explosive as the long-range, stepping blow.*

3. *Short range.* That's the head-to-head slugging range. You're at close quarters. You haven't room for straight punching. So you use *hooks* or *uppercuts.* Hooks are

FIGURE 17A

powered by the shoulder whirl or by a combination of the whirl and upward surge. Uppercuts are powered chiefly by the upward surge. The hook is a legitimate shoulder-whirl blow, and it can be just as explosive as a long-range straight punch. However, hooks usually are more easily evaded than straight punches. Uppercuts also can be extremely explosive, *if delivered correctly*. And a genuine uppercut is difficult to evade. You, or anyone else, should be able to hit harder with a hook or with an uppercut than with a medium-range, shoulder-whirl straight punch.

When you investigate the short-range blows, you'll learn why the ideal hook and the ideal uppercut would be

delivered at such close quarters that stepping would be impossible. However, I'd guess that about one-third of all hooks and uppercuts are delivered with a step, in order to reach a target that can't be nailed by a straight punch. But the step usually is so short that it doesn't enfeeble the blow.

While we're considering ranges and their blows, let me stress one extremely important fundamental: *a straight line is the shortest distance between two points*. Either fist, in its normal punching position, has less distance to travel *on*

FIGURE 17C

a straight line to its target than on the curve of a hook or an uppercut. Consequently, a straight punch always should be used when (a) it has just as much chance of nailing the target as either of the others, and (b) when it will be just as explosive as either of the others. In other words, don't be taking long steps with hooks or uppercuts when you should be sharpshooting with straight punches.

On the other hand, if you're in so close to an opponent that you're almost in a clinch, it would be silly for you to be rearing back and trying to stab your opponent's face with straight punches—when you could be exploding hooks or uppercuts on his chin, or digging them into his body. Your understanding of range will enable you to practise landing the correct blow for each distance. And it will help you to "judge distance"—to anticipate exactly where the chin of a moving head will be at a certain split-second. Also, it will help you in your "timing"—landing your punch at the exact split-second when your target reaches its designated spot.

Timing and judgment of distance are extremely important in a fight, where the range is changing constantly and you are using a variety of blows to suit the openings and the distances.

Chapter 14: Straight Punching from the Whirl

You give whirling motion to your body-weight by whirling the shoulders.

One shoulder whips forward while the other whips back. Muscles of the shoulders, back, stomach and legs co-operate in achieving the whirl. Also, the process is assisted by shifting the weight from one leg to the other. You need concern yourself only with the shoulder motions. Nature will supervise the assisting muscles and movements.

You can best understand the straight-punching whirl by feeling it out—without using a target.

Stand in the middle of a room with your feet even (on a sideways line) and comfortably separated. Place your relaxed hands in easy guarding positions before each breast (Figure 18). Turn your shoulders *easily to your own left* and, at the same time, extend your *right fist* to the chin of an imaginary opponent. As your *right fist* moves toward the opponent's chin, turn the fist so that it will land *palm-down*. Meanwhile, your *left shoulder* is well back, and your relaxed *left hand* is still in front of your left breast. Aim that *left hand* at the spot occupied by your extended *right fist*.

Now, *suddenly whirl your shoulders* TO YOUR RIGHT, *and let the shoulder-whirl shoot your* LEFT FIST *straight at the spot just occupied by your right fist.* Be sure you let the *whirl shoot your fist* instead of letting your projecting *left arm pull your left shoulder around.* As your *left fist shoots* at the imaginary target, *turn your hand so that the fist lands palm-down.* Meanwhile, your *right hand* returns to its relaxed guarding position before your *right breast*.

FIGURE 18

Practise that shoulder whirl on the bag. Shoot one fist, then the other—bang!—bang!—bang—BANG!—until you are striking out with a rhythmic motion of the shoulders. Your shoulders should be swinging back and forth like the handle bars of a bicycle. Do not move the feet. Be sure that you *explode* each punch. *Make certain that your shoulders are driving the punches; that the punches are not pulling the shoulders.* That position—with the feet on an even line—is ideal for throwing straight punches from the whirl. Unfortunately, however, that ideal position is not your normal punching position. Consequently, we'll have to return to your normal punching stance and try the whirling straight punches from that position.

In the middle of the room, take your *normal* stance, with your hands in normal guarding positions. Practise the shoulder whirl *easily* at first, without the bag. As your

FIGURE 19

shoulders whip from side to side, you'll note that your left leg acts as a *pivot*, above which your torso and shoulders whirl (Figure 19). If you toe-in slightly with the left foot, you'll get greater freedom in the *whirl from left to right—* the whirl that shoots out your *left fist*. And that particular whirl needs any assistance it can get. When you're in normal position, your guarding left shoulder is so well forward that you can't give it much whirl in shooting the left jab. You can't, unless you draw back the left shoulder. And if you do that, you may get your brains knocked out.

It's okay to use a *slight* toe-in with the left foot; but keep it *slight*. If you toe-in sharply, you may sprain or break your left ankle when you do the falling step. Moreover, the more freedom you give the whirl for your *left jab* with the toe-in, the less freedom you allow the reverse whirl for your straight *right*. That's true despite the fact that your left leg is serving as a pivot. *Each* SINGLE *straight punch of the whirling type—whether a lead or a counter—must be delivered from the normal punching position.* However, the instant you get into a rapid-fire, straight-punching exchange with an opponent, your good old *right foot again will come to the rescue.* That right foot will creep up until it's even or nearly even with your left. You'll be blazing away with both fists from the *ideal whirling position.* You'll be getting just as much whirl for your straight lefts as for your rights. Practise the *normal* and the *ideal* on the bag. *Whirling straight punches for the body are delivered in the same manner as those for the head.* The fists land palm-down.

You recall that in straight *stepping* punches to the *head*, the fist landed in an *upright* position, but that in *whirling* straight punches to the *head* the fist landed *palm-down*. Why the change?

The reason for the change is this: the average whirling straight punch *is not straight*. It's usually *looped* slightly or considerably. And the fist approaches its head target from at least a slight angle. Because of the angle, greater solidity is achieved by landing with the fist palm-down. Some instructors favour the palm-down landing for straight head blows "because turning the fist while in motion gives a snap to the punch." That's true. For a chap who doesn't know how to *explode properly*, that turning snap would inject a little dynamite into the blow. However, your explosion is not dependent upon a wrist turn.

What did I mean when I said whirling straight punches are *not straight*?

I meant that the non-step whirling straight punch is an *impure* punch, and that the harder you hit with it, the more nature tries to *purify* it by giving it a *loop*. I'll explain that.

Chapter 15: Purity in Punching

THE *stepping* straight punch, which you learned earlier, is *pure* because it has all the essentials of a punch. One of those essentials is this: *the body-weight must be moving in the same direction that your striking knuckles are pointing.* In other words, the body-weight must be moving in the same direction that the *exit* of your *power line* is *pointing.*

When you punch straight from the falling step, the fall and the right-foot spring send your body-weight *straight forward*—in the same direction your striking knuckles are pointing (Figure 20). And the assisting power you get from the accompanying shoulder whirl in the falling step *does not change the direction of your weight in motion. That essential*—same direction of weight and striking knuckles—*is lacking when you punch straight from the shoulder whirl,* WITHOUT STEPPING. You'll understand what I mean when you try this little experiment.

Take your normal punching position before the bag. Using the shoulder-whirl, hit the bag hard with your *left* fist; then, move to follow with a *terrific* straight *right* to the same spot. *But, instead of letting your right fist actually hit the bag, yank your fist in against your chest just before it can land.*

What happened?

Your body whirled around, using the left foot as a pivot. Your body had practically no tendency to *plunge forward* into the bag, for your weight was spinning like a top. Had you completed that punch, your *striking knuckles would not have been pointing in the same direction as that of your whirling weight.* Your striking knuckles were shooting

FIGURE 20

straight forward, but your shoulder was whirling. Usually when a straight punch is exploded against its target, the arm is fully extended. At the instant of explosion in a non-step whirling straight punch, the striking knuckles of the extended arm are trying to continue in *one direction*, whereas the shoulder is trying to pull the arm in *another direction* (Figure 21).

Your moving body-weight, instead of being exploded

FIGURE 21

straight forward into the target as it was in the falling-step punch, may be whipped away to the inside by your whirling shoulder. That type of punch *cannot have explosive follow-through*—unless your opponent steps into the punch. Incidentally, I believe that "whip-away" causes many of the mysterious shoulder and elbow injuries suffered by fighters—torn ligaments, pulled muscles, and socket dislocations.

The harder you throw a straight punch from the whirl,

75

the more your body will try to *purify* the punch by giving it *loop*. Your body will try to send your striking knuckles in the same circular direction in which your body-weight is whirling. The harder you try to punch, particularly in rapid-fire exchanges, the more old Mother Nature will try to force you to hook. You see: *the hook is the perfect whirling punch. It's pure.* Consequently, the more *loop* given a whirling straight punch, the more *explosive* the punch.

Nevertheless, you cannot let nature have her way with your straight whirls. It's unfortunate that the wider the loop, the easier your opponent's block or slip. Moreover, the straighter you throw your punches in a rapid-fire exchange, the better you will keep "inside" your opponent's attack. The fellow who has the inside track in an exchange usually lands the most punches. *So, don't loop 'em.*

Although a non-step straight punch from the shoulder whirl is *impure*, don't get the idea you shouldn't use the whirl for straight punching. *The whirl is very valuable when you can't step, and very valuable as an aid to power in the falling step.* The more power you can generate with the shoulder whirl, the harder you will hit with both types of straight punches; and the more explosiveness you will inject into your hooks. *The shoulder whirl is extremely important.* But let me stress this fact: *neither you nor anyone else will be able to hit as hard with a straight punch from the shoulder whirl* WITHOUT THE FALLING STEP, *as with it*. I emphasize that because many instructors teach: " Never step with a straight punch unless you have to." That instruction is wrong.

The trigger step (falling step) must be part of your instinctive equipment before you begin experimenting with straight, shoulder-whirl punches. Otherwise, when you do have to step with a shoulder-whirl punch, you'll be using the wrong type of step. When you step in with a left jab, you'll be using a *curved* step; you'll be letting your foot follow your whirl. And when you try to step with a straight right, you'll be trying to "hit off the right foot" by "raring back," like a baseball pitcher, before you throw the punch. A pitcher has time to rare back before he goes into his falling step, but if you rare back you'll be a "catcher."

You may ask, "Well, when should I step, and when should I whirl?"

The answer is simply this: *step with a straight punch whenever you get the chance, even if you can take only a very short step.* When you can't step, nature will force you to depend entirely upon shoulder whirl.

Let's move on to short-range punching: to hooks and uppercuts.

Chapter 16: Hooking

A " HOOK " is a whirl-powered blow that is delivered while the elbow is sharply bent (Figure 22A, B).

FIGURE 22A

Many people mistake a *swing* for a *hook* because each blow travels in a circular direction. There's a life-and-death difference between the two blows, however. That difference originates in the *hook's sharply bent elbow*. In the *swing*, the arm usually is fully extended, or nearly so (Figure 23A, B).

Although a swing is the most natural blow for a fellow

to use in self-defence, it is also the most treacherous blow that he can throw. The swinger leaves himself wide open to a punch from his opponent, both while he draws back to swing and while his fist is travelling in its long arc to the target. Moreover, since it's almost impossible for the fist to land with its *striking knuckles*, at the end of a hard swing, the landing usually is made with the palm-side knuckles or with the thumb knuckle or with the wrist. Any of those three landings is an invitation to a fracture. In addition, the

79

FIGURE 23A

swing is a doubly ineffective blow. It's easy for an opponent to block or to evade. And it lacks the explosiveness of the hook.

The *swing* lacks explosiveness because it's an *impure punch*. Although your arm *and fist* are travelling in the circular direction of your whirling body-weight, your striking knuckles are *not pointing* in that direction. Your striking knuckles—the exit of your power line—are pointing *straight out*, or nearly straight out. Your arm is moving like the spoke of a wheel; but your power line is running straight down the spoke and out of the end (Figure 24). *Unless your striking knuckles are pointing in exactly the same direction as your body-weight is moving, you will not have your weight behind the punch nor will you have frozen solidity along the power line when you attempt to*

FIGURE 23B

DIRECTION OF WHEEL

SPOKE

FIGURE 24

FIGURE 25

explode the punch. By bending the elbow sharply for the hook, however, *you point your striking knuckles in the same direction that your weight is whirling* (Figure 25). You achieve a pure punch. And the more sharply the elbow is bent, the tighter and more explosive is the hook. When you explode a hook against an opponent's jaw, you can feel your good old power line running just as solidly from shoulder through fist as when the line was straight out in a falling-step punch.

The hook is as pure as the swing is impure. To use the swing as a weapon in fist-fighting or in boxing is as dangerous as using a live rattlesnake as a weapon. The user is more likely to be the victim. And as far as the opponent is concerned, always remember this: Anyone who is so

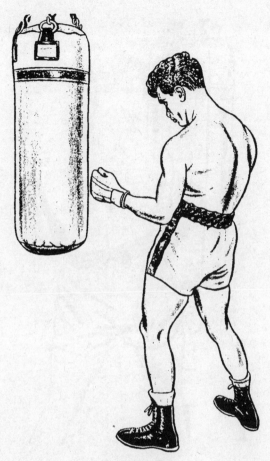

FIGURE 26

inexperienced or stupid that he can be hit by a swing is a palooka who can be "moidered" by straight punches, hooks or uppercuts.

Take the swing and toss it into the slop bucket and forget about it.

Let's examine those explosive beauties—*the hooks.*

Generally speaking, there are two types of hooks:

(1) *Shovel hooks,* which are thrown "inside" with the elbows "in," pressing tightly against the hips for body

FIGURE 27

blows; and pressingly tightly against the lower ribs for head blows; and

(2) *Outside hooks*, which are thrown with the elbows "out"—away from the body.

We'll feel out the "shovel hooks" first, for they are thrown from your normal punching stance and they are the short-range dandies you'll be using most in fist-fighting or boxing.

Take your normal punching stance before the heavy bag. Shuffle in close to the bag. Let your *left arm* dangle loosely at your side. Raise your *left hand* (thumb up) and your forearm until they are pointing straight out from your elbow (Figure 26). Pull your elbow "in" and press it firmly against the *front* edge of your hip bone. Turn your half-opened *left hand* up slightly so that your palm is partially facing the ceiling. Your palm should slant at an angle of about 45 degrees between floor and ceiling. Meanwhile, keep your *right hand* in normal guarding position. Now without moving your feet, *suddenly whirl your body to your* right *in such fashion that your* left *hip comes up with a circling, shovelling hunch that sends your exploding left fist solidly into the bag, about solar-plexus high* (Figure 27). The slanting angle of the *left* hand permits you to land solidly with your striking knuckles.

Try that punch several times. Make certain you have no tension in the elbow, shoulder or legs until the whirl is started from your normal position. *More important:* Make certain that (1) *Your hand is at the 45-degree angle,* and (2) *the hip comes up in a vigorous shovelling hunch.*

The "fist angle" and the "hip hunch" are important features of all shovel hooks, whether to body or head. The leg spring used in the hip hunch speeds up your body whirl and, at the same time, deflects the direction of the whirl slightly upward in a surge. Meanwhile, the combination of the angled fist and the bent elbow *points your striking knuckles in the same direction* as that of the whirl surge. You have a pure punch. Your fist lands with a solid smash that packs plenty of follow-through. *And your pure punch is angled to shoot inside an opponent's defences.*

Next, try a *right* shovel hook to the body. Use exactly the same combination of movements, but keep the *left hand* on guard. Because of the better shoulder and hip whirl you can get from the *right* side, the *right shovel* will be much easier for you to throw in the beginning. Practise a few rights.

85

Now we are ready to shoot shovels to the head.

Head-shovels are delivered from the normal stance at close range. If you have a pear-shaped, inflated punching bag, it will enable you to feel out the head-shovels more satisfactorily

FIGURE 28

than the heavy bag. That is so because your shovels are *rising* at chin-height.

Stand before either bag. Keep your hands in normal punching position. Fold the *left arm* in toward the body, keeping your forearm straight up until the thumb knuckle is only a slight distance from your *left* shoulder. Be sure that your *left elbow* is well "in" and that it is pressing against your lower left ribs (Figure 28). Now, without moving your

FIGURE 29

feet, suddenly give your body the combination shoulder whirl and hip hunch, and let your angled *left fist* explode the punch against your chin-high target (Figure 29).

Try four or five of those left shovels, making certain each

time that your elbow is pressing against the lower ribs, at the start of the whirl, and that your fist, when it lands, is only a short distance from your *left* shoulder.

If strangers were watching you practise that shovel to the head, one might remark, " Why, he's just clubbing sideways with his left hand." And another might say, " Naw, he's just throwin' a left uppercut."

Both would be wrong, for you are neither "clubbing" nor uppercutting. You are throwing a full-fledged inside left hook —one of the shortest, yet one of the most explosive, blows in the human arsenal. You're doing that if you're landing with your *striking knuckles,* and *not with the side of your hand.*

Next, try a few of the head-shovels with the *right hand.* These, too, will be easier to throw than the left head-shovels.

I permitted you to make certain preliminary moves or " telegraphs " when you were getting set to throw your first shovels to body and head. Later, however, after the combination of shovel movements becomes automatic, you'll not need to drop your elbows to your hips *before* starting the body punches; nor will you need to cock back your forearms and fists *before* starting the head blows. Instead, your hands will be in their *normal* positions before the blows begin. *But they will flash instinctively to their shovel posts as your body starts its hunching whirl. Your body will pick them up.*

You've probably been wondering how one gets into short range before throwing a shovel, since no step is taken with the punch. You won't have difficulty there. You can make the range, for example, with any number of attack combinations in which the shovels are used for follow shots. The simplest combination would be a long left jolt to the head, which failed to knock your opponent backward, *followed immediately by a right shovel to head or body.* Or, you could follow a similar straight left to the head with a left shovel to head or body. Likewise, a long straight *right* to the head, which failed to accomplish its explosive object, would put

88

you in position for *left* shovels to either target. Also, if a fast opponent steps into you, his speed may be such that you can't catch him with a stepping counter-punch; but that very speed may make him a perfect " clay pigeon " for your short-range artillery. In addition, you'll be in short range for counter-shovels many times when you ward off attacks by means of blocks, parries, slips and the like. I'll show you all the defensive moves later—after you've completed your punching education.

Practise the shovels until you perfect them. They are particularly valuable for the fist-fighter. In importance they rank next to your long, straight punches. They will enable you to knock out or at least " soften up " an opponent who is trying to clinch with you. They will help you, from your normal stance, to keep " inside " the attack of bobber-weavers, most of whom hook from the " outside." They'll help you to straighten up bobber-weavers, although not as effectively as will uppercuts. They'll eliminate the necessity of your " getting down " in a low crouch to try to beat a bobber-weaver at his own game.

Since the shovels are all short, tight blows, you are less likely to get hit while using them than while throwing the more open " outside " hooks.

That brings us to an investigation of " outside hooks."

An outside hook is any hook that's landed while the elbow is well " out " or " up "—well away from the body. The properly executed outside hook is a pure, full-fledged knock-out punch. Your striking knuckles are pointing in the exact direction of your whirling weight. However, the outside hook is *pure* only so long as you keep it *tight*—only so long as the elbow is sharply *bent*—only so long as it's delivered at *short range*.

Remember this: The more you " open " an outside hook, the more it degenerates into a *swing*. You must keep it tight.

Naturally that fundamental is true also of shovel hooks; but there's less tendency to open the shovels.

The amateur and professional rings are crowded today with "club fighters" who wade in with wild hooking attacks. Among them an explosive puncher is a rarity, for the club fighter's so-called hooks generally are so open that they're swings. Moreover, most of those club fighters are easy to nail because: *When you open a hook, you open your own defence.*

FIGURE 30

Let's try the *outside hooking* movement.

Stand in the middle of the floor, with your feet on an even line. Raise each elbow shoulder high, and bring " in " your half-opened fists, palm-down, until the thumb knuckles are pressing against your chest (Figure 30). The fists should nearly touch each other, but not quite. In that position, practise the easy shoulder whirl, letting each elbow and shoulder swing far back when the other elbow and shoulder

FIGURE 31

are forward. Keep your thumb knuckles lightly against your chest. Now, continue that shoulder-whirl practice; but, as each elbow whips forward, try to strike an imaginary chin-high target *sharply* with the *point of the elbow*. And, as you make your imaginary "elbow-point landing," clench explosively the fist that belongs to that elbow, while the fist's thumb knuckle is still lightly against your chest.

Next, go to the bag. Stand in the same ideal position, but close enough to the bag so that you can strike it with your elbow points (Figure 31). Hit it sharply six times with each elbow point. Then, as you are whirling to strike the bag the *seventh* time with your *left elbow point*, let your left fist come away from the body and smash into the bag at the same spot where the elbow point would have landed (Figure 32). Make your usual explosive landing with the second knuckle and with the fist palm-down. *Then, whip back and make the same sort of landing with your right fist.*

Practise a few of those fist-landings. Make certain that each hook is *almost as tight as if your fist still were against your chest.* And be sure you're *exploding* each punch. As you whip from side to side, it might appear to an observer that you're just in there swinging. But, brother, you aren't swinging. You're throwing *perfect punches*. Any one of those punches can knock an opponent stiff if it lands squarely on the *side* of his jaw.

Those are the kind of hooks you'll be landing in a head-to-head slugging exchange. By bending a bit lower you can *hook to the body—terrifically*. Your fists land to the body in the same palm-down position. Practise a few body hooks.

You have been throwing those outside hooks (to head and body) from the ideal hooking position or stance. You could get full body whirl for each fist because your feet were on an even line. And you could keep the hooks tight without much difficulty because you were close to your target. But as you shift to any other position you are immediately confronted with the problem of keeping those hooks pure. And you must use them in other positions, for they are too valuable as weapons to be restricted to the ideal stance.

In the *normal* punching position, the outside left hook is

FIGURE 32

very useful as a lead that shoots in behind the guarding right hand. And it is useful as a counter that "beats to the punch" a straight right started by your opponent. However, it is so difficult to get proper power into an outside left hook (without telegraphing) that the "corkscrew" is used. The late Kid McCoy, foxy old-time middle-weight, made famous the *corkscrew left hook*.

Try the *corkscrew* on the bag. Stand in normal position.

Do the following movements slowly: Start your shoulder whirl as if you were to shoot a medium-range left jab. No preparatory movement. Instead of jabbing, however, *snap your left forearm and fist down and your left elbow up.* Your left fist snaps down with a screwing motion that causes your *striking knuckles* to land properly on the target. When your fist explodes against the target, your forearm is almost parallel to the floor (Figure 33A, B). When you first try the corkscrew, the combination of movements will seem silly

FIGURE 33A

and futile. It will seem like a fizzle. With a little practice, however, you'll master it.

Let me help you at this point by admitting that the cork-screw usually is a medium-range punch, and that it's usually delivered while you are circling to your opponent's right. For that reason, it's nearly impossible to keep the corkscrew as pure—as tight—as the hooks you were throwing from the ideal position. Nevertheless, you can make the corkscrew

FIGURE 33B

explosive enough to stun an opponent, or at least to set him up for another punch. Moreover, if you have a potent *left corkscrew* that flashes in without warning, your opponent will be very cautious about menacing you with his *right* fist. Remember that your left hand, in normal position, is always closer to your opponent's head than his right hand is to your head. As he attempts to start a straight right, you can beat him to the punch with your countering corkscrew. Moreover, if he permits his guarding right hand to creep too far forward as he blocks or parries your left jabs, your corkscrew can snap down *behind* that guarding right and nail his jaw.

Can the left corkscrew be used for body punches?

Yes, it can be used effectively for landing left hooks to the right kidney or to the liver. It is best used, of course, after a feint to the head lifts your opponent's guarding right hand high. You use the cockscrew then as a lead. You can counter with a left corkscrew to the body, as you slip under a straight right. I'll explain " slipping " later. Let me caution you that it's dangerous to lead with a left corkscrew to the body, for your left side is open to right counters, and your head is in position to be nailed by a countering left hook.

Can the *corkscrew* be used with the *right hand*?

A right corkscrew to the head can be used properly only in one instance—as a counter-punch *after you have blocked an opponent's left hook with your right forearm*. At the instant the block is achieved, your *right fist* flashes down in a corkscrew hook to your opponent's *left jawbone* (Figure 34A, B). You can use a right corkscrew to the body as you slip under a *left jab*.

Thus far we have considered hooks thrown only when the feet are motionless—both shovel hooks and outside hooks; for hooks are purer and more explosive when delivered without a step. However, about one-third of all hooking openings can be reached only by stepping in, to bring the target within hooking range.

96

Always try to nail a long-range target (either body or head) with stepping straight punches. However, if your opponent is blocking, evading, or countering those straight blows, you can resort to long-range hooking attempts. *You can step in with any type of hook*, if necessary.

You'll step in most with the left corkscrew. But when you step with the corkscrew, you do not move in with the straight-forward falling step. Instead, you move in with a

FIGURE 34A

FIGURE 34B

"pivot step." You step forward and slightly to your own *left*, pointing the toe sharply in. Your body pivots on the ball of your *left foot* as your left arm and fist snap down to the target. At the instant of the fist-landing, your *right* foot generally is in the air; but it settles immediately behind you (Figure 35). If your opponent is using hooks that are "open" or semi-swings, you can step inside his left hook and land your own *right* shovel hook to his chin or to his body. In reverse,

98

FIGURE 35

you can step inside his *right hook* with your own *left shovel* to chin or body.

Usually when you slip a straight punch you can step beneath it with a corkscrew to the body. You can step in with hooks whenever you feel that the openings require it; but *don't let your stepping cause you to open your hooks so they become swings or semi-swings.* And once you do step in with a hook—regardless of its effect upon your opponent

—be prepared to let that hook be the first in a barrage of hooks, or the first in a combination series of hooks. In the *barrage* you merely blaze away to body and head, trying to land as many stunning hooks in the shortest time possible. The barrage may be shifted at any time from body to head, if it has brought your opponent's guard down; or, from head to body, if your opponent's guard has gone up.

Quite different is the *combination series*. The series has been practised many times in advance. It may include from three to six punches. Each punch has its particular target, and you try to make each punch find that target as you deliver them with rapid-fire speed. However, the chief aim of the series is that the combination of hooks, shooting for various targets, will so confuse your opponent that the target for the final punch will be wide open.

A series of five, for example, might be designed to open an opponent's chin for a crushing *tight outside hook* to the chin. Such a series could be thrown like this: (1) as you slip under his left jab, you smash him in the solar plexus with a right corkscrew, followed immediately by these outside hooks: (2) a left to the chin, (3) a right to the chin, (4) a left to the right kidney, and (5) a terrific right to the jaw. Sometimes you can mix shovel hooks and outside hooks in a series without destroying your punching rhythm.

Before I finish with hooks, let me tell you about an interesting punch called the "sneaker." The *sneaker* is a slightly overhanded right hook to the head, delivered at the instant you force a break-away from a clinch. In boxing, it is illegal for you to use this blow, or any other, *after the refeee has told you to break*. But you can use it before he orders a break—when you make your own break. In fist-fighting you can use it whenever you get the chance.

Here's what you do in a clinch when you haven't room to punch with either hand: (1) Keep your head in close to the *left side* of your opponent's head, with your chin slightly over his shoulder; (2) manoeuvre with your *left hand* until

100

you can grab the inside crook of his *right* elbow, and thus hold his *right* arm so firmly that he can't punch with it; (3) get his *left* arm under your *right* arm, and clamp your *right*

FIGURE 36

hand under his arm—just above the elbow—just below the biceps (Figure 36).

When you hold him in that fashion, he can't hit you; but you are in a perfect position to break away sharply and deliver a stunning overhanded " sneaker " hook.

Suddenly, yank him tighter to you with your *right* hand; then, shove him violently away with both hands; and— almost in the some movement—whip an outside *right* hook

FIGURE 37

up over his *left* shoulder—*and down*—so that your striking knuckles smash into his left jawbone or left temple (Figure 37).

If the "sneaker" is delivered properly, your opponent will drop like a poleaxed steer. If he doesn't drop, he'll be so groggy that one or two shovels to the chin will finish him. Practise the "sneaker" until you can do it automatically. It's called a sneak punch because it's delivered on the break, when an opponent is not expecting it, and when he's off balance. Because of its surprise and explosiveness, the *sneaker is one of the deadliest of punches.*

Chapter 17: Uppercuts

An "UPPERCUT" is a blow that shoots up straight (along an imaginary line from the floor) to an opponent's solar plexus or to his chin (Figure 38).

FIGURE 38

Because an uppercut rips up straight, it is very difficult to block or evade. It comes up *inside* the protections used against other blows—the guarding elbows, forearms and hands. An uppercut's direction differs from that of a shovel hook. The shovel sweeps *sideways* and up; but there is no sideways sweep to the uppercut. It shoots *straight up*.

There is an important difference between the deliveries of the two blows. All shovels are assisted by an *upward hunch* of the hip beneath the arm that is striking. *In the*

FIGURE 39

uppercut, however, the hip beneath the striking arm SHIFTS OR FADES ASIDE (Figure 39). The hip fades aside to permit straight-up gangway for the fist and arm. It shifts aside somewhat as does the hip of a man driving a golf ball. And the upward surge of body-weight is somewhat similar to that in the completion of a golf swing.

You'll understand the *fading* and *surge* by trying the following movements.

Face the heavy bag, with your feet about 18 inches apart on an even line about 18 inches from the bag. Bend your knees slightly. Bend your body forward slightly. Distribute your weight evenly on both feet. Teeter up and down to be sure you are comfortably balanced. Place the palms of your opened hands on the outside of your hips. Shift your weight easily to your *left* leg, letting your hips sway easily to your left (Figure 40). Still in slow motion, sway your weight to the *right* leg. As your *left* hip fades toward your right,

FIGURE 40

let your *left* hand slide forward off your hip and strike the solar-plexus spot on the bag easily with your fist *palm-up* (Figure 41). Sway your weight back to the *left* leg and let your *right* hand and fist go through the same sliding, striking motion, palm-up (Figure 42). Without trying to get any power into your punches, keep swaying your hips and using the sliding blows to the solar plexus until you feel yourself doing it with a sort of rhythm. Be sure that your fists are sliding *straight up* to the target. Be sure also that your hips are swaying far enough to let the elbows miss the fading hips on each punch.

Those are the fundamental movements of the uppercut. They must be done easily and automatically before you try to put dynamite into the blow, for the rest of the uppercut movements will seem outrageously awkward—at first. Okay, let's try the awkward moves.

FIGURE 41

FIGURE 42

Take your feet-on-the-even-line position before the bag.
Put your opened *left* hand on your *left hip*. But raise your
right hand to its normal guarding position. Your knees
should be slightly bent. Sway your weight to your *left* foot
so that you are resting lightly on the ball of your *right*
foot (Figure 43). Suddenly sway your weight to the *right*
foot so violently that your right heel comes down with a
thud. *And at the same time, wrench your* RIGHT *shoulder
and* RIGHT *arm upward so violently that your previously*

guarding RIGHT *hand flies up near the back of your head.*
Meanwhile, as your *left hip* faded to the *right*, your *left fist*
should have snapped straight up to the solar-plexus spot
with terrific impact (Figure 44). As the fist landed, your
weight should have been planted firmly on your *right* foot,

FIGURE 43

with only the ball of your *left* resting on the floor. Naturally,
your hips swayed far to the *right*.

Next, try a *right uppercut* to the solar plexus. Just before
you deliver the punch, your weight is firmly on your *right*
foot, and your opened right hand is on your right hip. Your
left hand is in normal guarding position. As you sway your
weight suddenly to the *left*, wrench your left shoulder and
left arm upwards and backwards so violently that your left
hand flies nearly back of your head. Meanwhile your *right*

FIGURE 44

fist shoots explosively straight up to the solar-plexus spot.
When you first tried that combination of uppercut movements, you probably felt you were working at cross purposes.
In delivering the left uppercut, you felt that shifting your
weight to the right foot had started your body-weight moving
to the right, and that the backward wrench of the right
shoulder suddenly tried to yank the body-weight in a
different direction. You will continue to feel that way until
you blend the movements into one unified motion. Then, on

FIGURE 45

the left uppercut, you will be: (1) hitting off the *left* foot; (2) dropping your weight so suddenly on to the *right* foot that the shift will act like the dropping of a weight on to the end of a seesaw, helping the spring of your *left foot* to give an upward surge to the *left side of your body*; (3) increasing that surge to include more body-weight by the backward wrench of the right shoulder.

Since your right shoulder will be pulling back, almost directly above your *left* hip, the surge will be almost straight *up*. In your first experiments with the uppercut I let you exaggerate the backward shoulder wrenches. I permitted you to straighten up and let your guarding hands fly back to the sides of the head. Naturally, you can't do those things in a fight. They would leave your head wide open to counter-punches.

Now, try the uppercut movements with just as much violence as before; but refrain from straightening up, and, under no circumstances, permit your guarding hands to fly away from their normal guarding positions (Figure 45).

In shooting uppercuts to the chin you'll naturally be more upright than when smashing to the body. The chin blows are delivered with exactly the same movements as those to the solar plexus (Figure 46).

You have been practising the movements by sliding your hands off your hips. Now, with your feet still on the even line, place *both* hands in normal guarding positions, and let each hand automatically drop into its proper route as it delivers the blow. Practise a few uppercuts in that position.

Next, try uppercutting from your normal punching stance. You'll find it difficult to get much power into the *left* upper-cut from the normal stance. Your *right* foot is back, and the hip-sway shifts your body-weight backward as you punch. *Consequently, the left uppercut should be used only when the feet are even or nearly so.* The *right uppercut*, however, is much more explosive from your normal stance than from the toes-even stance. Greater freedom for *right* leg-spring and *left* shoulder-wrench provides faster body-surge, despite the fact that the weight-shift from right to left foot is not as great as when the feet are even (Figure 47).

Uppercuts are particularly effective at close quarters against an opponent capable of blocking your various hooks to body and head or capable of bobbing under your hooks to head. The uppercuts explode *inside* his defences against hooks. They shoot straight up into a bobber's face.

Although most uppercuts are delivered at close quarters,

FIGURE 46

without moving the feet—without taking a step—*the right uppercut can be used effectively with a short step.* It can be used with a step as a *lead* to straighten up a croucher or bobber; and it can be used with a step as a *counter* inside an *opponent's* hook or swing. However, the *uppercut never should be used at long range—with a long step.* It is not a long-range blow. It opens; it loses its purity at long range. Moreover, it leaves you wide open when attempting to use it at long range.

FIGURE 47

Some current fighters attempt a long-range right upper-cut called the " bolo " punch. They even attempt to lead with it. Let me warn you that the *bolo* is more showy than explosive. It's more dangerous to the user than to his opponent. The bolo, or any long-range uppercut, is merely an underhanded swing. And you know that any type of swing, against a good straight puncher, signals to the mortician.

Chapter 18: Punch Ranks First

You now have a thorough understanding of "punch." Why did I give you such a detailed education in the fundamentals of hitting before I taught you any *defensive* moves?

I did it for many reasons, but the principal reason was this: The best defence in fighting is an aggressive defence. Each defensive move must be *accompanied by a counterpunch* or be *followed immediately* by a *counterpunch*. And you cannot counter properly if you do not know how to punch.

That does not mean that "a strong offence is the best defence." That overworked quotation may apply to other activities; but it does *not* apply to fighting. It does not apply when you're pitted against an experienced opponent. You may have the best attack in the world; but if you're an open target—if you're a "clay pigeon"—you'll likely get licked by the first experienced scrapper you tackle.

You must have a good defence to be a well-rounded fighter. And the best defence is an AGGRESSIVE DEFENCE.

Another reason for teaching punch first was this: you learned how to throw every important punch *without having an opponent attempt to strike you.*

I'm convinced that it's wrong to try to teach beginners punching moves and defensive moves at the same time. Most humans cannot have two attitudes toward one subject at one time. And a beginner can't have two attitudes toward fighting. If you take any ten beginners and attempt to teach them punching and defence simultaneously, more than half of them will concentrate on defence instead of punching.

That's a natural inclination, for it's only human that a

fellow doesn't like to get hit in the face—or in the body either, for that matter. It follows that more than half the beginners will consider it more important to protect their own noses than to concentrate on learning how to belt the other guy in the nose. They'll develop " defence complexes " that will stick with them. Fellows with defence complexes rarely develop into good punchers. Even when they are shown how to hit correctly, they sprout bad punching habits while concentrating on blocking, parrying, back-pedalling and the like. They " pull " their punches; they side-step while trying to throw straight smashes; they move in with "clutching " fists that seek to encircle their opponents for clinches; and they do much showy but purposeless footwork.

The little thought-ditch that is dug in the beginning will become the big channel for later fistic reactions. You're lucky. You're starting with the mental account punch. And it's a 100-to-1 shot that your attitude will not change. It's true that you haven't punched yet at a live target—at another fellow. Don't worry; there's plenty of time for that. And when you do start tossing at a live target, you'll know exactly how to toss. That exact knowledge will help you to become accurate and precise, as well as explosive, against a moving target.

Chapter 19: Your Sparmate

BEFORE you can learn the moves in aggressive defence, you must get a " sparmate "—some chap who can toss punches at you and who can be a target for your counter-punches.

In connection with that activity, let me give you a bit of advice. At the beginning of this book I pointed out that it was being written for any *healthy* boy or man—from twelve to thirty—who desired to learn to defend himself with his fists. It's natural that anyone who is neither crippled nor under a doctor's care should imagine himself to be healthy. And usually he is. However, just to make certain that you are physically okay for sparring, I suggest you have a doctor give you the once-over. The object of such an examination, of course, it to make sure that your heart will be able to stand a bit of strenuous activity. After getting the green light from a physician, go ahead and arrange for practice sessions.

If you're in a locality where you can practise in a gymnasium, you'll probably be able to find someone there who'll spar with you. I use the word " spar "; but you'll do no actual sparring during your first eight or ten sessions with a sparmate.

Use the early portion of each session to perfect your punching moves against a live target. Then, you can devote the latter portion of each session to defence. Follow that routine at each of your first ten sessions, at least. If you try to spar too soon—before your defensive and countering movements are learned correctly—you may develop bad habits, careless moves.

As you begin each defensive and countering with your

partner, *do it in slow motion* a few times before speeding it up. It would be best if your sparmate were a chap of about your own weight, although that is not essential in your early practice sessions. However, when you actually spar later *be sure* that your partner or partners are of approximately your weight. If you scale less than 175 pounds stripped, *never* spar with anyone who outweighs you more than twenty pounds, even though he may be a raw beginner.

If you register more than 175 pounds, try to limit your partner's advantage to thirty-five pounds.

In practice and in sparring make certain that both you and your mate use *big training gloves*—12- or 14-ounce gloves. Until you are an experienced performer, let no one tempt you to practice or spar with the 8-ounce gloves used in amateur tournaments, or with the lighter gloves used in professional bouts—five or six ounces. You can find the big gloves at almost any gymnasium, or you can buy them at almost any sports-goods store.

Do not bandage your hands for early practice and sparring. Unless you know a first-class trainer who can show you exactly how to wrap up your *particular* hands, forget about bandages and tape. Improperly bandaged fists are more likely to be injured than bare fists.

For protection against accidental low blows or knee raises, you should wear an up-to-date scrotum protector, made of tough fibre, leather and rubber. Such a protector can be obtained at a sports-goods store.

Don't worry about headguards and rubber mouthpieces until you're ready for amateur competition.

Wear regular boxing trunks and soft leather boxing shoes if you can get them. If you can't, wear an old pair of trousers and tennis or basketball shoes. Be sure they are *shoes* and *not slippers*. The shoe comes up around the ankle and helps prevent turned ankles. In either trunks or trousers, you can strip to the waist; or you can wear a shirt if you need warmth. If necessary, however, you can practise and spar in your regular clothes, right out in the street. *But make certain that you and your pal are wearing big gloves.*

Now that you have a sparmate and gloves, we'll begin the study of defence.

Chapter 20: General Defence and Blocking

FOR our purposes "defence" means this: how to prevent a starting punch from landing on its target, and how to counter with a punch.

Punches thrown at you by an opponent will include blows aimed for head or body with either hand. They can be swings, hooks, uppercuts or straight punches. They can be prevented from landing on their targets by three methods: (1) *complete evasion* of the blow by slipping, bobbing, pulling away or side-stepping; (2) *deflection* of the blow by parrying (brushing away) with the hand, or by knifing with the forearm, or by shrugging off with the shoulder; (3) *blocking* the blow solidly with the hand, forearm, elbow or shoulder.

Evasion is the preferred method. When you force an opponent to miss completely with a blow, he usually lurches off balance and leaves an opening for your counterpunch. Moreover, since the blow has not touched you, it has not off-balanced you for counterpunching.

Deflection is the next best; for the parry, glance or shrug usually off-balances your opponent without interfering with your own equilibrium.

Blocking is the least desired; for a solid block not only affects your balance but it also may bruise the spot that makes blocking contact with your opponent's fist. Repeated bruisings of one spot—for example, the left shoulder muscles—can handicap your fighting. Nevertheless, *blocking must be learned first.* It is much easier for the beginner to *block* than to deflect or to evade.

We'll start with *blocks for straight punches to the head.*

The straight *left* is blocked by your opened *right hand* (Figure 48). Take your normal punching position before your sparmate. Let him lead at you with a slow-motion *left jab*. Your guarding *right hand* should flash "in"

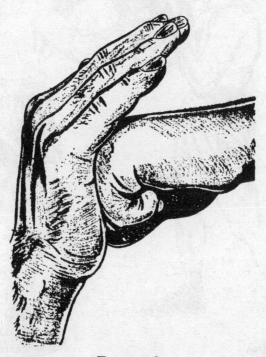

FIGURE 48

slightly and catch your mate's fist in your open palm, as near the heel of your hand as possible (Figure 49). Be sure that the block is so *solid* that the jab doesn't force your hand back into your face.

Keep your eyes open when you're making the block. Never close your eyes; no matter what kind of a punch is coming at you, and no matter what kind of a punch you are throwing. Keep your eyes riveted on his *left fist.* After you develop the habit of watching punches, you'll discover that even though your eyes are focused on one threatening

FIGURE 49

fist, you'll be noting from the corners of your eyes every other move your opponent is making.

Block several of your mate's left leads in slow motion. Then let him speed up the jabs. Be sure you're not changing your punching position as you block, that you are not trying to step back or to pull away from the jab.

Next, you'll block that left jab and you'll *counter at the same time*. Watch your mate closely. When he *starts* a left

FIGURE 50

jab at you, step into him with your own *left* jab to his face, and *at the same time* block his jab with your *right hand* (Figure 50). Shoot your *left* so fast and hard you'll *beat him to the punch*. Your *left* fist should land and knock him off balance as you block the blow. The objective is to *hit him just a split-second before his fist smacks into your hand*. By so doing, you'll bring into violent collision on the chin: (1) your forward-moving body-weight, and (2) his forward-

FIGURE 51

moving body-weight. That's the aim of most counter-punches: *catch him coming in*; hit him not only with your weight, but also with his own.

Practise that fundamental block and counter until you can do it automatically, with power and accuracy. Be sure you are using the falling step and that your *left* fist is landing in an *upright* position.

Next, let your mate try blocking your left leads, and

FIGURE 52

countering you with his *left*. Your alert *right* hand must block his *left counter*—as you step in—in the same fashion that it previously blocked his left lead. If your *left lead* is fast and hard enough to knock him off balance, despite his block, his *left counter* will be weak. Or he may not be able to counter.

Some expert defensive boxers use a "bump block" against a left lead. The *right* hand blocks with an *upward* motion, and the heel of the hand *bumps* the left lead up into the air over the head or shoulder. However, that's too fancy and dangerous for us. If you're fighting a chap who's fast enough with his left lead to outspeed your left counter, be satisfied to block it without making a fancy right-hand movement that might deflect the blow into your face.

Straight right leads to the head are blocked by either (1) the extended *left* hand, or (2) by the hunched *left* shoulder.

FIGURE 53

The extended *left* hand does the blocking if the lead is thrown at you when you are in normal punching position. Let your mate throw a *right lead* at you in *slow motion*. You step in and block or " smother " his right fist with the heel of your opened left hand before his right lead is well under way (Figure 51); and, at the same time, shoot your own straight *right* at his chin (Figure 52). If, however, his right lead is thrown at you when you are out of normal

FIGURE 54

position—when, for example, you have permitted your left hand to drop down in an overzealous feint to the body—you must block with your *left shoulder*. You give your left shoulder a frantic, whirling hunch to protect your already snuggled chin. Thus, the blow thuds into your shoulder instead of into your face (Figure 53).

You'll be tempted to use your *right hand* to help your left shoulder in that block. You'll be tempted to make a

FIGURE 55

"shell defence" with shoulder and hand. *But don't do it.*
You've got to keep that *right hand* in its normal position,
ready to (1) guard against the possibility of a following
left hook, and (2) smash a straight *right* counter to your
opponent's solar plexus or chin.

Straight punches to the body are blocked with the elbows.
To block a straight *left* to the body, the body is turned
slightly to the left and the punch is caught with the right

FIGURE 56

elbow (Figure 54). To block a *right*, the body is turned to the right so that the left elbow catches the punch (Figure 55). By using the elbows instead of the forearms for body protection, the hands can be kept in nearly normal punching and guarding positions. Blocking a straight *left* to the body, you can counter with a left shovel hook to the chin (Figure 56). Blocking a right to the body, you can counter with a right shovel or a right uppercut to the chin (Figure 57).

FIGURE 57

Blocking hooks and swings: Left hooks and swings to the head are blocked with either the *right forearm or the rigid, opened right hand.* Blocking contact is made with the *outside edge* of the arm or hand. The longer and wider the blow, the more easy the block. If the punch is a *left* swing or *left* hook used as a lead, you block with the *right* forearm or hand, and *counter simultaneously with a left jab to the chin* (Figure 58). If the punch is a tight *left hook* at

FIGURE 58

FIGURE 59

close quarters, you block with *right* hand or arm, and counter simultaneously with a *left shovel* to the chin (Figure 59).

Right hooks and swings to the head are blocked with the *left* forearm, hand or shoulder. At long range, you counter with a straight *right* to the jaw; at close range, with a *right shovel* or uppercut.

Hooks to the body are blocked with elbows—keeping

FIGURE 60

the hands in punching position. You can counter with shovels or uppercuts to the chin.

Uppercuts to head or body are blocked by dropping your *forearm or hand* on to the opponent's upshooting fist or forearm. You may be able to counter with either a regular outside hook, or an overhanded hook thrown like the " sneaker " (Figure 60).

Chapter 21 : Deflection

DEFLECTION " is achieved by (1) " the parry," and (2) " the glance-off."

The *parry* is used against *straight punches for head or body*. Let your mate throw a *left* jab at your head. Your opened *right* hand whisks in and gives him a brisk slap on the wrist, forcing his *left* jab to pass over your left *shoulder* (Figure 61). The parry or " brush-away " is done without

FIGURE 61

great effort, without interfering with your balance. However, the deflection spins your opponent off balance and leaves him open for your countering *left shovel* to solar plexus or heart. Next, have your mate lead at your head with a straight right. Whisk his wrist with your opened left hand, so that his right goes over your right shoulder—or to the right of the shoulder (Figure 62). Counter simultaneously with a *straight right smash* to the body or with an outside *right hook* to the body.

Parries for head blows are used *only in that manner*. Do not attempt to "cross-parry" head blows. Do not try to reach across and whisk a right lead with your right hand, or a left jab with your left hand. The instant you attempt to cross-parry, you leave yourself open on the side of your cross-parrying hand.

FIGURE 62

FIGURE 63

Some boxers attempt to parry straight punches to the head *from the inside out*. I mean they use a whisk of the right wrist to send a left jab over the right shoulder. That can be done, but the method is dangerous against a fast puncher. In the first place, your guarding hands are not in position to give proper outer whisk. The punch is likely to break through. Secondly, you are risking broken thumbs, for the outward whisking movement throws your thumbs up into prominence.

If one wishes to use an outward movement, it's far better to choose the powerful chopping or knifing back-handed " glance-off " that deflects the blow with the outer edge of hand or forearm, instead of with the whisking back of the hand.

FIGURE 64

Straight punches to the body are parried with the brush-away from the *inside to the outside*. Let a mate shoot a *left* at your body. The *right* hand and *forearm* whirl down, inward, and then outward, whisking your opponent's wrist *away to the right* (Figure 63). As you execute that parry, you step in with a *left shovel* to the jaw. When your mate leads with a straight *right* to the body, reverse the procedure and whisk with your *left* from inside to outside (Figure 64). You counter with a right shovel or right uppercut to the jaw.

The glance-off is even more important than the parry in causing deflection. The guarding positions of your hands and arms, and the hunched *left* shoulder in your normal punching stance were designed to give the upper portion of

137

FIGURE 65

your body a wedgelike effect. That wedging of hands, arms, shoulder and forehead should enable you to (1) keep inside an opponent's attack as you step in to lead or to counter, and (2) cause most blows to glance off to the sides or up into the air.

The glance-off is more dependable than the parry because there's more solidity, if necessary, in the glance-off than in the parry. The reserve solidity is there only in case your glance-off has to be turned into a block. However, the less solid the glance-off, the less your own balance is disturbed. Your glance-off movements are not the solid, chopping movements of hand or arm blocks; they are lightning, knifing or sliding movements. They interfere little with your balance, but they spin your opponent slightly out of punching position.

FIGURE 66

If you watch a professional fighter punch the light bag, you'll note that more than half his bag-work comprises a rhythmic tattoo achieved like this: straight left—backhand left—straight right—backhand right—straight left—etc. You may ask, " Why this backhand striking, when the backhand blow is illegal in boxing? "

The answer to that is: He's sharpening his backhand for glance-offs and blocking. If you get a chance to use the light bag, spend half your time on that tattoo. A powerful backhand for glancing and blocking is almost as useful for a fighter as is a good backhand for a tennis player.

The glance-off against left leads: If your opponent throws TRULY STRAIGHT left jabs at you, it will be difficult and dangerous to try to knife them to the outside. The *right hand-block* is a much more certain defence; and the *parry* would be more dependable than the *glance-off*. However, if the left jabs are slightly angled or looped (as in the case of most), the *glance-off* can be used effectively. You knife off the *left jab* with the *side of your rigid right hand* or with the *side of your right forearm* (Figure 65). *Remember:* Whether you block or glance off a left jab, you counter simultaneously with your own straight left.

The glance-off against right leads is achieved by knifing with the *left hand or forearm* (Figure 66). That's an excellent protection, because your guarding left hand is normally inside his right. His body turns slightly in throwing the right. Naturally, it's better for your knife-edge to contact the opponent's wrist or forearm instead of fist. Practise knifing *right leads* and stepping in with your own *right* counters to the face or to the heart.

Note that when you attempt a right lead of your own, your left hand and arm should be in a position to knife off a countering *right.*

Although glance-offs work perfectly against slightly looped straight punches, they should not be used against swings or hooks. Be content to block swings or hooks if you can't evade them. You'll learn " evasion " now.

Chapter 22: Evasion

" EVASION " is the method of defence whereby you force an opponent to miss a punch *without any physical contact.*

It is the preferred method because it throws an opponent off balance without interfering with your equilibrium. It opens him up, but allows you complete punching freedom.

" Evasion " is achieved by (1) *slipping,* (2) *bobbing,* (3) *footwork,* and (4) *pulling away.*

A *slip* is the evasion of a straight punch to the head by *shifting the head to either side of the punch,* and letting the punch *slip over a shoulder.* To understand the theory of the slip, try this experiment. Stand in normal position and let your mate lead a *very slow-motion straight left* at your chin. Instead of trying to defend by blocking or parrying, do not change the position of your hands. Merely *tilt your head to your right as far as possible.* Try to let his left fist slip over your left shoulder. That wasn't successful, was it?

If one were able to do this trick by simply tilting the head —without moving shoulders or body—he would achieve the perfect slip. Unfortunately, however, humans are so constructed that it's nearly impossible to get the *left side of the neck and jaw* out of the path of a straight punch to the chin, even when tilting the head to the *right.* And when you try to let a punch slip over your right shoulder by merely tilting your head to the left, you discover (in normal position) that your head has no room to tilt to the left because of the protective left shoulder.

Accordingly, the head must have assistance in slipping a punch. That assistance is provided by *rolling the shoulders.*

FIGURE 67

In fact, the shoulder roll will do all the work in shifting your head. *You need not try to tilt your head even slightly.* And that's fortunate; for when you tilt your head to either side, you find difficulty in keeping your eyes on your opponent. Moreover, when you side-tilt your noggin, you immediately change the head-and-neck angle of greatest resistance to a punch—the angle you use in your normal position.

Let's try the slip.

Have your mate throw a *slow-motion* left jab at you. As the punch starts, you roll your *left* shoulder forward and down, as if you were about to deliver a left corkscrew to the body (Figure 67). That movement will succeed in

FIGURE 68

making your opponent's left pass harmlessly over your left shoulder, as you slip to the outside. Practise that slip ten or twelve times without attempting to counter. As you become accustomed to the slipping movements, your mate can speed up his jabs.

Next, try slipping the *left jab* over your *right* shoulder. Use a similar forward and down roll with that shoulder (Figure 68), as you slip to the inside. Try that defence ten or twelve times.

Now you are ready to counter on slips against *left jabs*. Return to the *left shoulder* (outside) *slip*. On each slip, step in with a *left corkscrew* to the body (Figure 69). Try that counter several times. Make sure that you begin your cork-

FIGURE 69

screw as you begin your slip. Then return to the *right shoulder* (inside) *slip*, and counter with *right corkscrews* to the body (Figure 70).

When countering left jabs with corkscrews to the body, considerable *down* roll may be used. However, the down roll must be slight when you slip a left jab and counter with a " right cross " to the head.

The right cross—deadliest of all counterpunches—is used when a left-jabber becomes careless and forgets to keep his chin protected by his left shoulder as he jabs. Try the *right cross* like this: As your mate throws a *slow-motion left jab* at your face, slip the punch over your right shoulder

FIGURE 70

(inside); but, as you slip, step in and *shoot a straight right counter over your mate's extended left arm to his chin*. It is called a *cross* because it crosses his extended arm (Figure 71).

The right cross is a terrific blow because (1) it is entirely unexpected, and (2) it crashes into your opponent's jaw as he is coming in. The punch packs the fast-moving weight of *both bodies*. The straighter you keep the cross, the more explosive it will be. Many fighters make the mistake of hooking the cross. Many also err in delaying the counter until after their opponent's jab has slipped over the shoulder.

Don't make those mistakes. Keep the cross straight, and shoot it in the same split-second your opponent starts his jab. To do that requires enough practice to give you nearly perfect timing. And when you use it in a fight, don't throw it until you are positive that your opponent *is* exposing his chin when he jabs.

I stated earlier that a well-rounded fighter is always in position to punch—that you do not have to *get set* to punch. That's true. But in using the cross, you must get set mentally, at least. You must anticipate your opponent's jab. That is, you must watch him and time him until you're certain he's ready to jab again. Then, *let him have it!*

The right cross is used only as a head-counter and only against a left jab. Never attempt to use a left cross (if there is such a thing) as a counter *when slipping a straight right.* Trying that, you may get your brains knocked out. You wouldn't have slipping room between your left shoulder and your chin.

Slipping straight rights, you use movements similar to those employed in sliding under straight lefts. Counter with corkscrews to the body, but never attempt a left cross. You can slip inside or outside on straight rights.

However, remember this: *In slipping either a straight right or a straight left, you'll be safer if you slip the punch over your left shoulder.* The *left* shoulder-slip moves your head into a sort of " safety zone," where it would be difficult for your opponent to hit you with either fist. In other words, it's more dangerous to use your *right* shoulder for slipping either inside a left jab or outside a straight right, than it is to use the *left* shoulder for slipping either outside a left jab or inside a straight right.

When a *left jab* goes over your *right shoulder*, your head may be in position to be nailed by a following right uppercut or right shovel hook. And when you try to slip a *straight right* over your *right shoulder*, there's always the risk that

FIGURE 71

you may roll solidly into the punch. Nevertheless, you must be able to use right-shoulder slips against either of an opponent's fists. Often the action in a fight will force you into a position where you must use the right-shoulder slip. For example, if an opponent has feinted you into attempting a left-handed block or " muffle " of his right, it would be very awkward for you to try to let the right slip over your *left* shoulder when he *does* throw it. Instead, you must slip it over your right shoulder. You would be in a somewhat similar position if you were short with your own right counter to the head, and had to slip either a countering left or right. Moreover, there are times when you can do greater damage with *right smashes to the body* on *right shoulder-slips* than with the other combination. For example, if your opponent telegraphs his right, or if he is slow in starting it, you must be able to slip outside that right and paralyse him with your own right smashes to the solar plexus. And, of course, you must be able to slip inside his left jabs in order to deliver your own right cross.

Some fighters who never learned to hit on the slip, use *delayed counters*. For example, a fellow slips a left jab over his right shoulder without hitting. Then he is in position to counter with a right hook to the body; but he also is in position to be nailed on the chin by his opponent's right uppercut. Had he delivered the body-smash on the slip, his opponent probably would have dropped the right hand instinctively to protect the body, leaving the opponent's chin wide open for a left shovel to the head.

When you hit on the slip, you not only take advantage of the immediate opening, but your damaging blow forces a defensive gesture by your opponent's free hand, and thus makes another opening. *Always hit on the slip!*

Bobbing might be called *glorified ducking*, for a "bob" is an artistic duck. To most folk the word "duck" when applied to human movements, means a frantic, undignified downward dodge to escape being hit by some flying object. And that's what a "duck" usually is. But such is not the case with a "bob." There's nothing frantic nor undignified about the bob. When executed properly, it's as graceful and controlled as a bow from the hips made by lucky Alphonse as he kisses Chérie's hand. And why not? After all, the bob *is* a bow. And please don't let it be anything else.

You'll understand the "bow" business when you use the bob to evade swings and hooks for the head. Let your mate throw a slow-motion swing at your head with either fist. Before he swings, be sure you're in normal punching position, with your weight forward as usual. As he swings, merely bow forward from the hips. That is: you merely relax your back and stomach muscles and let the upper part

148

FIGURE 72

of your body jackknife down and forward, *without moving the feet*. The knees bend only slightly more than normally (Figure 72). As you start to bow beneath the swing, your knees may try to take a big dip. That's natural. It's instinctive to try to squat down with the legs when you're ducking anything. But don't do it. *Be polite. Merely bow.*

The purposes of the bob are: (1) to sink under the swing or hook with a *single, perfectly-controlled* movement; (2) to bring your fists in toward your opponent; (3) to maintain nearly normal punching position with legs and feet,

FIGURE 73A   FIGURE 73B

even at the bottom of the bob; and (4) to maintain at all times your normal slipping position with head and shoulders, for defence against straight punches.

It's extremely important that you be *in position to slip at any stage of the bob*. Your freedom to slip will enable you to employ the " bob and weave " in attacking. I'll explain the *bob and weave* in a minute. Meanwhile, try a few more bobs under your mate's slow-motion swings. Make your bow from the hips naturally and easily, and without throwing your weight so excessively forward that you will off-balance yourself. Keep your hands in guarding positions.

FIGURE 73C   FIGURE 73D

Generally, you will not be able to counter on the actual bob, if it's a straight-down bob that's not part of a *weave*. But you'll be in position to make delayed counters at the bottom of the bob with whirling straight punches to the body or with outside hooks. Or, you'll be able to come up from the bob throwing terrific right or left shovels to body or head. Practise the bob a little every time you spar until its movements become automatic. However, don't practise it too long at any one session, before the muscles of your left hip and leg become accustomed to the strain that bob-

FIGURE 74A   FIGURE 74B

bing from the normal stance puts on them. Your muscles
may get stiff and sore.

Now, we'll return to the *bob and weave*.

A simple *weave* is merely a series of *slight, imaginary
slips*. As you shuffle forward toward an opponent, you roll
your left shoulder slightly; then your right; then your left;
etc. (Figure 73).

The objects of the weave are (1) to make a moving target
of your head (from side to side); (2) to make your

152

FIGURE 74C   FIGURE 74D   FIGURE 74E

opponent uncertain about which fist you will throw when you punch; and (3) to make your opponent uncertain about which way you will slip if he punches at you.

When you are using the weave *by itself* in your normal punching position, you must keep your shoulder movements *slight*. Otherwise, you'll open up your defences. However, *the weave is rarely used by itself.* Almost invariably *the weave is used with the bob.*

Do a slight *bob-weave* like this: In normal position, bob slightly. As you come up from the bob, roll your *right shoulder* forward. As you swing back from that roll, bob again. As you rise from the bob, roll your *left shoulder* forward; then back, and bob, and right, etc. You'll quickly get a rhythm to that combination of movements so that they can be done without effort (Figure 74).

FIGURE 75A   FIGURE 75B

When the bob is used with the weave, your head becomes a more elusive target, and the uncertainty increases as to whether you will evade a punch by bobbing or slipping.

Nearly all fighters use the bob-weave to some degree as they shuffle towards their opponents. Most of them use it *mildly*. However, the genuine bobber-weaver uses it *fully*. He uses a deep bob and a wide sway (Figure 75A, B, C, D, E). He uses it to slide under his opponent's attack. He uses it to

FIGURE 75C   FIGURE 75D   FIGURE 75E

get to close quarters; the real bobber-weaver always is a hook-ing specialist. If he slips in under a straight punch, he hits on the slip and continues with a terrific barrage to body and head. If he bobs in, he begins his barrage with a delayed counter to the body.

Experienced bob-weavers often use the " apple bob " with great effectiveness. It is done like this: As a left jab starts towards you, you make a quick, *low*, combined slip-bob to the outside; and, in the same motion come up on the out-side (Figure 76A, B, C). The entire movement—slip, bob, rise —is *circular*. Your head appears to go down *inside* your opponent's arm and to bob up like an apple or a cork *outside* the arm.

In the *apple bob* you do *not* counter on the slip. Instead, you counter as you rise. You counter with a left *shovel* to the chin. The shovel is delivered while your opponent's *left arm* is over your *left shoulder*. And, the instant your shovel lands on his chin, you *follow* with an overhanded " right sneaker " hook to the jaw. A reverse combination of counters can be used when you apple-bob *outside* an opponent's straight right.

Because of my varied fighting experience before I reached Toledo, I was—or should have been—a well-rounded fighter when I faced Willard. Nevertheless, I specialized in the bob-weave attack. It was only natural that I should, for it is the perfect attack for one to use against taller opponents. I was comparatively small for a heavyweight, and I found the bob-weave very effective against larger men.

No one *taught* me the bob-weave. I picked it up the hard way. Charley Diehl, one of my schoolmates at Montrose, developed into a pretty fair fighter. He might have gone far in the ring, but he preferred the range as a chef. Anyway, I noticed that Charley was a very elusive target because he approached in a *deep crouch* and because he kept swaying from side to side. And I noticed that when he got into striking range, his right foot crept up and well off to the right of his *left foot*. I mean his feet were separated more than those of most of the fighters. I practised Charley's style quite a bit; but that deep crouch made me very tired. Guess I was bending my knees too much.

It was a good thing for me that I practised it. I used that deep-crouch and sway against a huge negro named " The Boston Bearcat " in a fight at the Alhambra Theatre in Ogden, Utah, in 1915. He was big and powerful, and he had a mule-kick punch. But I didn't let him hit me. I figured my only chance was to *slide in* with Charley Diehl's crouch and sway, and " tear his insides out." That's what I did, and it worked fine. I started smashing the Bearcat in the solar plexus and never stopped until he was on the floor —in the first round.

That unexpectedly quick victory gave me tremendous respect for the crouch and sway. I began analysing it to see what "made it tick"—to find out exactly *why* it was so hard to hit a fellow when he was using that defensive approach. I discovered that I was actually making *slipping* motions as I swayed, and that it was those slipping motions that made my head an elusive side-to-side target. I wasn't using any regular *bobbing* motion at that time; but I realized that being in the low crouch enabled me to sink easily under punches. I began experimenting with the bobbing motion and found that it made my head more elusive. I can't recall when sports writers began calling my combination of movements the "bob and weave." But I do know this: I had never heard of the bob and weave when I fought The Boston Bearcat in 1915.

One valuable defensive asset of the bob is this: A straight-punching opponent not only has to direct his blows downward to reach your head, but he has to be very cautious lest he hit you in the forehead and break his hand.

There are two ways to fight a bobber-weaver: (1) Get down and bob-weave with him, and (2) work on him from your normal position with shovels, uppercuts and straight one-two's.

The first method is better *if you can bob and weave as well as your opponent.* However, if he's a specialist at the bob-weave and you aren't, you'll be handicapped because you'll be trying to beat him at his own game. If you haven't developed into a proficient bobber-weaver, you'll do better from your normal stance; although that stance does leave your body somewhat open to attack by a bobber-weaver.

Using either style against a bobber-weaver, remember this: Most bobber-weavers become careless with their *rhythm*, and you can *time* their movements. You try to nail them with uppercuts as they sink into bobs, or with shovels as they start back from sways. When you use the bob-weave, *watch your rhythm.* As you near an opponent, *break your*

rhythm. For example, instead of continuing to use the series of slipping and bobbing movements that you can do with least effort, make slight bobbing movements as you sway from side to side; then sway twice to one side with deep bobs; then a slight bob in the centre; then two deep bobs on the other side, etc. Break your rhythm so that it will be difficult for your opponent to time you.

In using the bob-weave, you'll find that when you come within striking range of your opponent, your *right foot* will creep up until it is nearly on an even line with your *left foot.* That position will give you greater freedom in weaving and

FIGURE 76B

it will give you greater freedom in using your left hook for
a simultaneous or a delayed counter-smash to the body as
you slide in. *Footwork provides another method of evasion.*
You learned the fundamental step of footwork during your
study of punching—the falling step, the forward and backward shuffles, the side-step, the circle, and the pivot step
for corkscrew hooking. You learned the fundamental:
Make the *first step* in any direction with the foot already
leading in that direction.

When the side-step is employed to evade a punch,
do *not* try to counter while taking the step. Some
boxers counter on the side-step; but they get no power into

FIGURE 76C

their counters, for their punch isn't moving in the same direction as their body-weight. Wait until you complete the step; then throw a delayed counter from the normal position.

Do not confuse the defensive side-step with the important procedure of *stepping inside* punches. When you step inside a punch, you counter terrifically as you step. Here's the

FIGURE 77A

way to *step inside*: Have your mate take a slow-motion *left* swing at your head. You step straight inside the swing. As you step, you punch for the chin with the *right hand*—either straight, shovel or uppercut (Figure 77A, B). The swing

FIGURE 77B

FIGURE 77C

FIGURE 77D

FIGURE 77E

FIGURE 77F

should circle harmlessly around you. Next, have your mate throw a slow-motion *right swing* at you. Step in and punch with your *left hand*. Then, let your mate shorten his swings into hooks, and practise stepping inside them at close

FIGURE 78

quarters. You'll find that tight shovel hooks to the chin are the best counters when you step inside hooks that are fairly tight. (Figure, 77C, D, E, F.)

Note that the punching procedure when stepping inside

FIGURE 79

IS JUST THE REVERSE *of the procedure used when blocking and countering.* When you *block* a left swing with your *right*, you *counter with your left.* But when you *step inside* a left swing, you *punch with your right*, without making any block. You can hit harder when stepping inside a punch than when you block and counter or parry and counter.

The last and worst type of evasion is the pull-away. Some

168

FIGURE 80

fighters call it the " snap-back " or " snap-away." It can be
used with or without a back step.

Try it first without the step (Figure 78). As your mate
shoots a *left jab*, you sway backward from the waist, shifting your weight to the *right foot*. That should cause his
jab to fall short, and it should leave you in position to

169

counter with your own left jab. Next, take a back-step as you *pull away* (Figure 79).

The *pull-away* should be used only as a last-resort defence against straight punches or uppercuts. *But never try to pull away from hooks or swings to the head.* You'll be pulling *right into them.* Know how to use the pull-away; but don't get the habit of using it. If you keep alert, you can employ any of the more effective defensive movements you've already learned. If you get the habit of pulling away from *straight punches*, you'll instinctively try to pull away from *hooks and swings.* Remember this: It's just as *dangerous* to try to pull away from a *hook* or a *swing* as it is to try to hit an experienced opponent with a *swing*.

There's one more evasion, which I wasn't even planning to mention because it's so dangerous that it's really not a defence. It's just an invitation to disaster. It's called the "drop-away." As your mate shoots an overhanded *right* at you, you move as if to slip it over your *left* shoulder; but, at the same time, you take a short side-step with your *right* foot and let your body bow down over your *right knee* (Figure 80). That movement is designed to make the overhanded *right* fall short of its target. However, it's too dangerous for any intelligent fighter to use. Your dropped *left* arm provides poor protection for the left side of your body; and your head is a ready target for your opponent's left hook. Moreover, you are completely out of punching position; you can't deliver a counter.

There's one move that might be called a half-defence. That's the "head roll." You roll the head *when you're getting hit.* You roll the head when it's too late to do anything else. At the split-second when you realize you're going to get hit with a *right hook* or a looping straight *right*, you roll your head to your *right*. Moving your head *with* the punch will eliminate some of the blow's explosiveness and may make the fist *glance off* the side of your face or jaw. You roll to your own *left with an opponent's left hook*.

If you're getting nailed with a genuinely straight punch, do not roll your head back. You can let your body do an instinctive pull-away; *but keep your head in its normal position—chin down.* If you try to roll your head back, your chin will come up, and—blooie!

Chapter 23 : Feinting and Drawing

I WARNED you earlier against using "light stuff" to make openings or to set up opponents. I stressed that you took just as much of a gamble when you tapped an opponent with a left jab as when you hit him with a left jolt that might knock him down. Any time you extend your left fist to an opponent's head for a tap or for a jolt you may be countered with a left jab, a right cross, or hooks on slips to the body.

Note also that there's a big difference between *making an opening* and *setting up* an opponent. When you make an opening you merely cause an opponent to uncover a target somewhere on his person. But when you set up an opponent, you knock him off balance with one punch so that he should be an open target for a following punch. Unless he's knocked off balance, he's not set up.

And you do not *necessarily* set up an opponent by landing a light left jab on his face or forehead. Many an experienced fighter will let a light jabber land several lefts on his face. The experienced fighter will not be set up by those jabs. Instead, he'll merely be getting ready to go boom! on the light-jabber's jaw. He'll be "sucking him in."

Instead of using *light stuff*, you (1) *make openings* by feinting and by drawing, and (2) *set up* opponents by landing explosive jolts that knock them back on their heels.

What is a "feint"?

A feint is a threatened or faked punch that is not delivered.

What is a "draw"?

A draw is a faked opening left for your opponent to punch at, so that when he punches *he* will leave an opening at which you can counter.

How is the feint used?

The feint generally is used to create an opening, although it can be used either to prevent an opponent from punching when he's set, or to draw an opponent into punching.

To create an opening, you threaten a punch by making a telegraph with the fist, shoulder, knee, foot or eyes. For example, if you wish your opponent to uncover his *chin* by dropping his guard, you might make a slight jabbing motion with your left hand toward his body. Or, you might make a slight roll with your left shoulder toward his body. Or, you might suddenly shift your eyes to his body. Yes, so slight a telegraph as an eye-shift can sometimes cause an opponent to punch.

If you wish to "open" your opponent's *body*, you do your feinting at his head. Some fighters feint with the left foot. They smack the left foot down as if stepping. You shouldn't do that. It's dangerous to foot-feint, for when you lift the left foot you disturb your body-weight and your punching position. When feinting with your hands, particularly for the body, be careful not to extend the hand *too far out or too far down*. Such extensions will leave your head unguarded.

Shoulder feints are the safest and best.

With practice, you'll discover that you can feint an opponent into making any number of moves. You can feint him into slipping, so that he'll be a target for a shovel. You can feint him into bobbing toward an uppercut. And you can feint him into disclosing what defence he will use against any particular blow. When you become an expert feinter, you can force an opponent into fighting *your* fight. You can induce him to make moves that will open him up —moves that will disclose whether he will block, parry or slip a punch; moves that will prevent him punching when he's set; moves that will prevent *you* from wasting punches and leaving needless openings.

173

How is a " draw " used?

You *draw* an opponent into punching at you by leaving an intentional opening. It is a faked opening because you not only are aware of the gap but you are prepared to counter your opponent *before he can take advantage of the opening.* For example, you can draw your opponent's left jab by carrying your right hand so low that your chin will be exposed. You know you are exposed, but you are set to counter with a right cross or with a slipping body hook at the split-second he starts his jab.

Similarly, you can draw a straight right lead by dropping your left hand. Or, you can raise an elbow on either side to draw a lead to the body. You can drop a hand or raise an elbow in feinting and draw him into punching at the opening. *But make certain that your draw doesn't boomerang on you—that you don't get hit instead of your opponent.*

In connection with faking, I'll tell you about an attacking combination that may prove useful. It is called the " double shift." It's for use against a retreating opponent. You do the *double shift like this* (Figure 81): Telegraph that you are about to shoot a *straight left* at your opponent's head. Shoot the left, which he'll evade by stepping back. Then, immediately strike forward with *your foot,* and (as you stride) shoot a straight *right* at the head. If he's fast, he'll avoid that one too, but narrowly. Then, immediately stride forward with your *left* foot and (as you stride) shoot a straight *left* at his head. Put everything you've got into that last left, for it's nearly certain to nail him.

The double shift is designed to force a retreating opponent to (1) step back from the first left, and (2) immediately spring away frantically to avoid the unorthodox right that should (3) leave him flustered and unprepared to avoid the final unorthodox left. It is called the " double shift " because your body is shifting to the southpaw stance as you throw the *right* and shifting back to the normal stance as you

174

FIGURE 81A

FIGURE 81B

FIGURE 81C

FIGURE 81D

FIGURE 81E

shoot the last *left*. The combination of movements should be made with utmost speed and savagery—with your fists going whoosh!—whoosh—*boom*! Even if you miss him with the last left, you'll be back in normal punching position, ready to work on an opponent who should be extremely flustered.

Some fighters use the double shift with hooks instead of

straight punches. The late Stanley Ketchel, a "wild man" slugger, used the shift with overhand swings, landing on the side of an opponent's jaw and neck with thumb-knuckle and wrist. Stanley must have had cast-iron hands. I would advise you not to attempt the double shift with hooks, for your long strides will open the hooks into swings or semi-swings. Moreover, use of the hooks will leave you dangerously open as your body turns at the beginning of each shift.

Chapter 24: Training

TRAINING has two objectives: (1) to condition your body for fighting, and (2) to improve your workmanship as a fighter.

Although some exercises help condition and others speed improvement, there's one all-important activity that assists *both*. That activity is sparring.

There is no substitute for sparring. You must spar regularly and often to become a well-rounded scrapper, regardless of what other exercises you may take. Sparring not only improves your skill, but it also conditions your body for fighting by forcing your muscles to become accustomed to the violent, broken movements that distinguish fighting from any other activity.

Much has been written about *rhythm* in fighting. Nearly every scrapper develops some rhythm to his movements in footwork, bobbing, weaving, etc. And some " fancy Dans " appear to have almost as much rhythm as a ballet dancer when they shadow-box. But when the *chips are down, rhythm is destroyed*. Your opponent's feints, leads, counters and defensive moves will break your rhythm in a hurry and will force your movements, on attack or defence, to be necessities of the split-second—to be violent and broken.

Because the movements in fighting are violent and broken, *fighting is perhaps the most tiring of all human activities*. Some college experts insist that rowing in a crew is more exhausting than boxing. I don't know about that. I never rowed in a crew. But I do know that crewmen have a rhythm or " beat," to which they time their strokes.

A fellow may be a perfectly conditioned athlete for some other activity—like basketball, football, baseball, rodeo, riding, acrobatics, hurdling, wrestling, etc.—but if he hasn't had sparring practice, he will be completely exhausted by one or three minutes of fast fighting. His muscles will be unaccustomed to the movements, and he will be unaccustomed to breathing while making those movements and while being hit.

For a beginner, at least, *sparring is the most important conditioning activity*. Sparring also is the most important "sharpening" activity. It perfects your timing and judgment of distance in punching against a live and elusive target. It makes you adroit on defence and alert in countering. It grooms you to make exactly the right combination of moves in a split-second instinctively.

Shadow-boxing is the next best exercise for the twofold purpose of conditioning and sharpening. It might be described as fighting an imaginary opponent. It is particularly helpful in developing footwork. Although most professional fighters do not use boxing gloves during their shadow work, beginners should use them. Their weight will help to develop stamina. As you shadow-box, go through the same offensive and defensive movements you use in sparring. To be most valuable, your imaginary fighting should be done at top speed. Too many scrappers loaf at this work.

Bag-punching is another exercise that conditions and sharpens. At every practice session you should work three rounds on the light, inflated bag, and two rounds on the heavy "dummy" bag. Speaking of rounds, I advise that in your early training—sparring, shadow-boxing, bag-punching, etc.—you limit each round to two minutes. Rest one minute between rounds. Later you can extend each round to three minutes, the same time used in rounds in professional fights and for rounds by professionals in gymnasiums. However, continue to limit each rest period to one minute.

Work on the bags will develop all the muscles you use in

punching, and it will give "tone" to them. Your chest, shoulders and arms will take on that sleek, well-rounded appearance that distinguishes the bodies of most fighters from those of ordinary chaps.

Work on the light bag is more important than that on the heavy bag; for the light bag is a speedy target that

sharpens your timing and judgment of distance, as it conditions your muscles. Before each session of light-bag punching, you should make certain that the bag is about chin-high and that it is *firmly attached* to its topboard. If it becomes unscrewed from the topboard while you're punching you may get struck in the face by the metal attachment. If your bag is too low, the topboard will be too low; and you may strike the board with your fist if you miss a punch. On some punching-bag standards, the board can be lowered or raised. However, if the board is stationary, the gymnasium

FIGURE 82B

proprietor usually provides a small, wooden platform, five or six inches high, on which a short chap can stand and be in proper position to hit the bag.

Devote one minute of each round on the light bag to the straight-and-backhand tattoo. You do that tattoo in your normal punching position without moving the feet. The tattoo goes like this: straight left—backhanded left—straight right—backhanded right—straight left—backhanded left, etc. (Figure 82a, b). That exercise not only develops your muscles and timing for punching from the whirl, but it also gives you a powerful blocking or slicing backhand. During the other minute (or two minutes) of each round, you should practise all your head blows—stepping straights, fast medium-range exchanges, shovels, corkscrews, tight outside hooks, and uppercuts. Be careful not to strike the topboard with your uppercuts. *Hit the bag hard. Don't get the habit of using light stuff, even on the bag.*

The heavy bag serves two purposes: (1) It accustoms you to landing *solidly* with every type of punch to head or body, and (2) it provides a body target that's lacking in light-bag work. Practise all your punches on the dummy, and use the proper footwork when you do. Spend about one minute of every round in sharpening your bob-weave attack. Slide in with corkscrews to the body; then barrage the body terrifically with hooks; next, lift the barrage to the head. The next time you slide in, try a mixed barrage in which one fist smashes the body and the other the head; then the head-fist to the body and the other to the head, etc. Practise combinations series after you slide in.

Use your own striking gloves on both bags. If you use some other fellow's gloves and skin your knuckles, you may get your hands infected. Put camphor ice on your skinned knuckles before you go to bed. In a few weeks your knuckles will become calloused, and you'll have no more trouble with them.

Good exercises for conditioning the body are roadwork, rope-skipping, and calisthenics.

Roadwork means running on the road. Running strengthen the legs and develops stamina. It also takes off weight if your wear warm, heavy garments while running. Regardless of other apparel, you must wear shoes that have sturdy soles and tops that come up over your ankles. Also, you should wear heavy socks to prevent your feet from becoming blistered. If you are soft and poorly conditioned when you begin training, you should harden yourself by hiking over rough ground for at least two weeks before attempting any running. When you do begin to run, take it easy at first. Limit yourself to dog-trot jogs of about a half-mile each morning for seven days. Then, gradually increase the distance until you are jogging about two miles.

After you've become accustomed to roadwork and your feet have hardened, mix up your runs by sprinting for 100 yards, then jogging, then shadow-boxing for a few seconds, then jogging, then sprinting, etc. Nearly all professional fighters do their roadwork early in the morning. Do yours whenever you get the chance. Naturally, you'll take a shower when you come in from your spin. Professionals do from three to ten miles on the road.

Rope-skipping develops stamina, co-ordination and leg-spring. At a sports-goods store you can buy a skipping rope (not one of those toy ropes that kids use). Or, you can make a rope by soaking a piece of clothesline overnight in a can of light lubricating oil. Hang up the rope and let it dry out for a day. Then, fold the ends of the rope back and tape them into " handles " with bicycle tape. The skipping rope should be fairly heavy but not too thick. That's why you give it the oil treatment.

In skipping, you do not jump with both feet at the same time; nor do you skip with a hippity-hop, like a school girl. Instead, you bounce off one foot and then off the other (Figure 83). That will seem awkward at first, but soon you'll be skipping with an effortless grace that will surprise you and your friends. To make skipping interesting, you can learn to do it backward. You can learn to cross the rope forward and backward, and to make the rope go

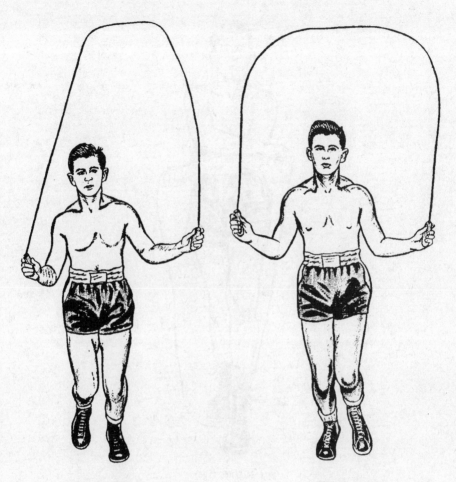

FIGURE 83A   FIGURE 83B

around you twice while you are in the air once. You'll have
a lot of fun with the rope. You'll be able to do footwork
while skipping, and perhaps you'll even be able to dance a
jig while the rope is whirling about you. Naturally, the
skipping is done in a gymnasium or in whatever you are
using for a gym. Do at least two rounds of skipping at each
workout.

FIGURE 83C

Calisthenics for a fighter are exercises designed chiefly to build up protective muscles in his stomach and neck, and to make him supple. A fighter should avoid heavy exercises like weight-lifting, for they tend to make him muscle-bound.

Bending exercises are best to develop the stomach muscles into a protective "washboard" against body blows. The best bending exercise is done while lying on your back on a

186

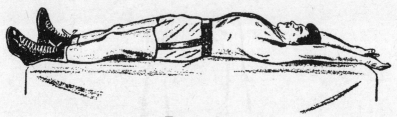

FIGURE 84A

reasonably soft surface such as a mat or several thicknesses of towels. Lie stretched out flat with your feet together and your arms extended back of your head (Figure 84A, B). Bend forward slowly, bringing your hands up in an arc, and touch your toes with your hands. Then return slowly to your original stretched-out position. If your feet rise when you bend forward, have someone hold them down. Repeat the bending until you are tired. At first, you'll tire quickly; but in a few weeks you'll be able to do 25 to 30 bends; later, 50 to 100.

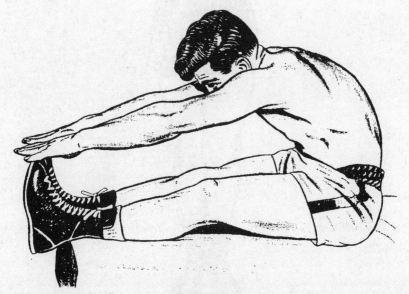

FIGURE 84B

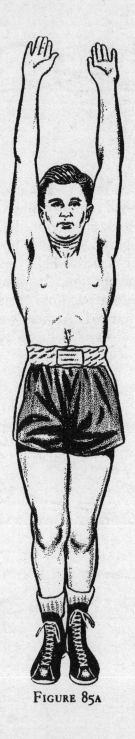

FIGURE 85A

FIGURE 85b

You can break the bending monotony by spreading your legs and touching the *left* toes with your *right* hand; and on the next bend, your *right* toes with your *left* hand, etc. Also, you can lock your hands behind your neck and, in that position, bend forward until your chin goes between your knees. Keeping your hands in that position, touch your *left* knee with your *right* elbow on one bend, and your *right* knee with the *left* elbow on the next one, etc.

Be certain you do those bends on a soft surface so that you cannot injure the vertebrae of your lower spine. *In a standing position*, you can go through practically the same bends (Figure 85a, b). Keep your knees stiff while doing them. However, the bends are much more beneficial if done while lying down, for then the stomach muscles are required to do more work.

FIGURE 86A

Neck muscles should be strong to absorb the shock of head punches. The best exercises for *strengthening the neck* muscles is the " bridge " (Figure 86). Lie on your back on the mat. Lock your hands on your chest. Make a simple *bridge* by raising your body until it is supported by your feet and your head. Still in the simple bridge, roll back on your head until your forehead is touching the mat. Then return to the simple bridge, and then to your stretched-out position. Repeat the procedure several times. You can also strengthen the neck muscles while you are standing. Turn the head from side to side, and on each turn stick out the chin as far as possible toward a shoulder.

There are many other exercises you can learn around the

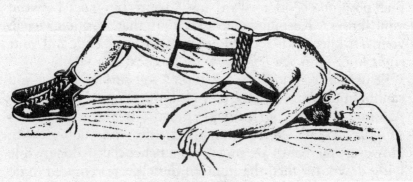

FIGURE 86B

gymnasium that you can use if you decide to go into amateur or professional competition. But those I've given you are plenty to help you become a well-rounded scrapper.

For example, you can develop strength in your arms and shoulders by using wall pulleys, and by doing "push-ups" from the floor. Some trainers do not approve of the pulleys or the push-ups. They believe those forms of exercise tend to make you muscle-bound. I approve of them, unless you already are heavily muscled in the shoulders and arms.

You can strengthen your hands *outside* the gymnasium by carrying with you a rubber handball and squeezing the ball for a couple of hours each day, first in one hand and then in the other. I advise that, if your hands are fragile; for strong durable hands are very important in fighting. Strong hands help your explosions and also help prevent bone-breaks.

Some trainers harden the stomach muscles of their fighters by throwing a medicine ball at their stomachs. The fighter stands with his arms relaxed, and lets the ball hit him squarely in the body. He catches the ball as it bounces off his stomach, and returns it to the trainer for another throw. That's a good hardening procedure for a fellow who's already had two or three years of training. But I wouldn't advise it for the average beginner. You might injure yourself internally.

Every boxer—beginner or seasoned professional—must have a gymnasium schedule and a general schedule for the day, and he does best when he sticks to those schedules.

After you've had six weeks or two months of preliminary, informal training—while learning punching and defence, and practising them in sparring—you might adopt a gymnasium schedule like this:

Shadow-Boxing ...... two rounds
Sparring .... three rounds
Heavy Bag .... two rounds
Light Bag .... three rounds
Rope-Skipping ..... two or three rounds
Calisthenics .... two rounds

Take a one-minute rest between rounds. Having finished your workout, you take a five-minute " sweat-out " by sitting relaxed or by lying down in the dressing room. In either case, you are warmly wrapped in your bathrobe or in a sheet. Make certain you are not in a draught.

After the sweat-out, take a quick, lukewarm shower. If the workouts make your muscles stiff and sore, you should take a rub-down after the shower. Most professionals take a rub after each workout, as insurance against soreness and to keep their muscles supple.

The " rubber " (rub-down man) applies soothing lotions to the muscles as he kneads them with his fingers. You doubtless will not have the services of a rubber while you are learning to fight. However, you might arrange for your sparring pal to rub you down in return for your rubbing him. You lie on your back on a rubbing table or on towels on the floor and let him work on the front muscles of shoulders, arms and stomach; then, turn over and let him knead the rear muscles of shoulders, arms and legs.

If you can't make an arrangement like that, you can apply rubbing lotion to your own muscles after each session—if you need such treatment. You can make your own rubbing preparation by mixing the following: 3 ounces of rubbing alcohol, 3 ounces of witch hazel, 1 ounce of wintergreen, and 1 ounce of olive oil.

If you have engaged in a particularly violent sparring session or in a bruising fight, you can prevent soreness in muscles and bruises by taking an Epsom salts bath at home. Fill a bathtub nearly to the top with very warm water, and pour in five pounds of Epsom salts. Lie in the tub half an hour. Then go to bed.

All professionals do their gym work in the afternoon; but most amateurs have to do theirs at night, because most amateurs have jobs in the daytime. High school and college boys are exceptions, of course. They usually can do their gym work in the late afternoon. Regardless of when you go to the gymnasium, and regardless of whether you're an amateur or a professional, you should do your roadwork early in the morning.

Here's a good daily training schedule for an amateur who has a job:

6 A.M.   Rise. Drink a cup of hot tea, or a cup of beef broth or chicken broth.

6:30 A.M.   Hit the road.

7 A.M.   Arrive home. Take brief sweat-out and shower. Have breakfast of fruit juice, cereal, eggs, and milk or tea.

12:30 P.M.   Lunch of lettuce and tomato on toast (perhaps with two or three slices of bacon). Glass of milk or cup of tea. If you do not have bacon with the lettuce-tomato sandwich, you can drink a malted milk.

6 P.M.   Gymnasium. Have cup of hot tea with lemon before the workout.

7:15 P.M.   Workout completed.

7:45 P.M.   Home and dinner: half grapefruit or glass of fruit juice or cup of broth. A salad with olive oil and perhaps lemon juice. No vinegar! Meat —anything broiled or boiled; nothing fried. Steaks, chops or chicken. Stews are good if you need to gain weight. Also, a baked potato, if you need weight. But no pork, veal, lobster, shrimp, crabmeat, or starchy foods like spaghetti.

For dessert: stewed fruit, prunes, apricots, pears, or rhubarb, etc. Also hot tea. No pastries.

8:15 P.M.   Relax half an hour.

8:45 P.M.   Take a fifteen-minute walk.

9 P.M.   *Bed.*

The amateur's diet is about the same as that of a professional; but the pro's schedule is much easier from the angle of time. The pro is on the road at 5:30 A.M. Returning to camp, he can rest until 10 A.M., when he has breakfast. when he loafs until noon, when he can have lunch or a nap, depending upon his weight. He begins his gym work at 2:30 P.M. Then he relaxes until dinner at 5 P.M. or 5:30 P.M. After that more loafing or a movie until 10 P.M., when he goes to bed.

An amateur who is training and working on a job, at the same time, must make sure that he gets eight or nine hours' sleep every night. Otherwise he may go "stale." He may become listless—"dopey"—on his job, and off-form in his sparring. He burns up much energy every day, on the job, and on the road and in the gym. He must get more than eight hours of sleep in twenty-four to restore his energy. And he should sleep with his windows open. He can't get oxygen—he can't recharge his batteries—by sleeping in a closed room.

I neither smoked nor drank before I became champion. I would not preach to others that they likewise should refrain from tobacco and alcohol. However, I believe that my avoidance of smoking and drinking gave me that extra bit of stamina which enabled me to win several hard fights by the narrowest of margins.

If you are in an area where no trainer or instructor is available, I suggest that when you go to your doctor for a physical check-up, before attempting to spar, you also have the physician decide whether your weight corresponds properly to your height, bone structure, and age. Don't let any of your friends tell you, for example, "You should weigh about 155 pounds because you are five feet ten inches tall." Your weight depends considerably upon your bone structure. You might stand only five feet seven, yet properly weigh 200 pounds, if you were big-boned and broad-shouldered—husky but squat. You could be a six-footer, yet properly weigh 165 pounds or even less if you were slender and small-boned. Moreover, if you happen to be a youngster in the fast-sprouting state, you could be skinny and all bones and joints, but still be normal.

Your weight is very important. If you're too soft and flabby, you should pare off some poundage by exercise and proper diet, so that your body will be firm for fighting. And if you're too skinny, exercise and wholesome food will help build you up. Find out from your doctor about how many pounds you should take off to be at your "best weight," or how many you should put on.

Though you resemble a circus fat man or a human skeleton, you'll be able to fight surprisingly well if you practise the fundamentals of explosive fighting I've explained in this book. You'll be able to stiffen many a fellow with one punch, or with a couple of punches. But remember this: You'll be able to fight better if you make your weight conform to your height and bone structure. Excess fat will slow you up and make you get winded in a hurry. Also, it will prevent your developing protective stomach muscles. On the other hand, if you're skinny and undernourished, you will not be able to hit as explosively as if you had your normal weight. Punches to the body will weaken you more than they should, and you will tire more quickly than you should.

Weight is ultra-important in fighting. Get your right weight; make the proper use of it; and you'll have happy, explosive landings.

Chapter 25 : How to Watch a Fight

Boxing is the perfect spectator sport. It's easier for anyone to watch and understand a fight than to appreciate what's occurring in any other type of sports contest. That's true whether one witnesses a bout at a fight club or on television.

Only two men participate in a fight. All the action occurs under bright lights in a space about twenty feet square. Generally, one need have no knowledge of boxing to determine which scrapper appears to be winning. Nevertheless, if *y-o-u* wish to get complete entertainment from a fight, you should do more than sit down "cold turkey" and watch it.

Despite its primitive simplicity, a fight is similar in at least one respect to most other kinds of sports contests: the more you know about the rivals, the more you'll enjoy the competition. If you plan to witness a professional bout—at a fight club or on television—learn in advance as much as you can about the two fighters. Read the sports pages of your newspapers; you'll probably find advance stories about the show. Pre-fight stories usually provide sufficient information not only to stimulate your interest but also to make you favour one of the leather-tossers. You'll work up a rooting interest in the engagement. While reading the stories, note first the betting price. When you read, for example, that Johnny Brown is favoured at 8 to 5 to beat Billy Green, you get a "quick picture" of the bout in advance. The price shows that more money is being wagered on Brown than on Green and that betting men, at least, consider Brown superior to Green.

Note next the reasons why Brown is favoured. Did these

two fight before? Did Brown win? Has Brown an advantage in age or in weight? Is he a mature and experienced performer of twenty-five or twenty-six facing a comparatively green youngster? Or, is he a chap still possessing the sparkle and stamina of youth, pitted against a veteran of thirty or thirty-one who is on the "toboggan?"

Perhaps Brown is favoured because of his more explosive punch or because of his superior speed and cleverness. Perhaps Brown's record shows he has been meeting and beating a better grade of opposition than Green has been facing.

Do the boxing writers pick Brown? They do not always agree with the betting price, for they know that its "quick picture" is often as false as it is quick. I have no statistics on upsets, but it's my belief that the underdog in betting wins about one of every three important fights.

Is each of the contestants a local boxer, or is one from a distant city or from a foreign country? Has he been in your area long enough to be accustomed to the climate?

What do the stories say about the private lives of the contestants? Is either a playboy who prefers taverns and nightclubs to gymnasiums for his training? Remember that successful fighting requires nearly perfect condition. Ring history shows that a few playboys—Mickey Walker, Stanley Ketchel, Maxie Baer, Maxie Rosenbloom, Ken Overlin, etc. —were able to get to the top; but they were exceptions.

Is there anything about the personal appearance of either fighter that makes you favour him? Usually the papers carry pictures of the principals before a bout.

Before you sit down to watch the fight, decide which boxer should win or which one you hope will win. That should help to give you a rooting interest. However, do not let that rooting interest cause you to make a mistake that is common to most fans and many officials. Because of their interest in one of the fighters, they watch the scrap only from *h-i-s angle*. They watch the punches he lands or receives. Their eyes unconsciously see the action as follows: " Brown landed two left jabs to the mouth. Brown was hit by a left hook to the body. Brown landed a right to the cheek. Brown ducked under a left hook, etc."

Instead they should be seeing the action like this: " Brown landed two left jabs to the mouth. Green landed a left hook to the body. Brown landed a right to the cheek. Green missed with a left hook to the head."

The big secret of correct fight-watching is this: keep your eyes and your attention focused on *both* men—not on just one. If you watch from the angle of *one* fighter, it's almost certain that you'll overestimate his performance without realizing it. You'll unconsciously emphasize the punches he lands and minimize the number and effectiveness of his opponent's blows.

Watch both men, even though you strongly favour one of them.

When the action starts—when the gong sends them out of their corners—note the physical appearance of each. Does the appearance of your favourite bear out his pre-fight descriptions, or does his opponent seem more formidable? Note immediately their fighting styles. Are their styles similar or do they contrast sharply? Are both upright boxers, or does either use the semi-crouch or the low bob-weave?

Which one is pressing forward—forcing the fight? That's important; for in a close contest the aggressor usually is the winner. However, if the aggressor fails to land his punches and is hit with counterblows, his forcing them is a handicap instead of an advantage.

Which one appears to have the superior left jab? Is he using it merely to " paint " with, or is he jabbing solidly enough to snap back his opponent's head and knock him off balance? Is his opponent blocking or slipping those jabs, and is the opponent countering them with jabs, right crosses, or body smashes?

Which has the superior left hook? How is he using it? Is

he keeping it short enough to be explosive? Is it accurate, or is his opponent bobbing beneath it or stepping inside it? If neither principal is a knockout specialist, the one who is more effective with the left jab and left hook probably will win.

Has each enough confidence in his own punching ability and ruggedness to engage the other in toe-to-toe exchanges? Or, does the lighter puncher shrewdly avoid exchanges by left-jabbing or by footwork or by covering up when the slugger is bombarding him? It's folly for a comparatively light puncher to permit himself to be lured into exchanges with an explosive hitter. However, when the slugger's barrage has ceased, the lighter puncher must begin an immediate attack upon the slugger—before the latter can get set for another bombardment.

If both scrappers are willing to fight it out in exchanges, the bout should be thrilling. Watch the early exchanges closely; for what happens in them may indicate the ultimate winner.

Does one appear to be hitting with more speed, accuracy and power in the exchanges than the other? Is he " rocking " his opponent, knocking him sideways or back onto his heels? Is he hurting his opponent not only " upstairs " but also in the body? Has either begun to bleed from the brow, cheek or mouth? Often an old face-gash will be re-opened in an early exchange. Remember that if the opponent makes a target of a cut and hammers it until it bleeds profusely, the referee may stop the bout and give victory to the opponent on a technical knockout.

Less important is a bloody nose. Rarely is a bout stopped because of a bleeding nose: not unless the blood flows so freely that a nose haemorrhage is indicated.

Note carefully when either man is hit hard enough to be staggered. There's a big difference between being " rocked " and being " staggered." When a fighter is rocked, he is knocked violently off balance—backward or sideways; but he still has complete mental and physical control when he recovers his balance. When he's staggered, he loses temporary mental and physical control—in varying degrees. Usually his knees sag and he becomes " rubber-legged " as he lurches about the ring. Sometimes a big black blob seems to gush up before his eyes, and he can't see for a second or two. And sometimes his arms are semi-paralysed, and he can't lift them to protect himself from follow-up blows. Sometimes he is completely groggy.

If a fighter is staggered, watch closely to see how badly he is hurt. Can he raise his arms for protection? Can he see his opponent and try to fall into a clinch with him, to give the groggy mind a chance to clear? Make up your mind about the staggered man's condition in a split-second; for his opponent will be after him quickly for " the kill "—for the knockout. Often one solid shot to the chin will floor a staggered fighter for the full count of ten.

However, rugged scrappers of the Tony Zale type can take a terrific head battering, even when reeling helplessly from rope to rope, without going down. Others can quickly shake off the effects of a staggering punch, and can regain control soon enough to defend themselves before being nailed again. Usually a fighter is staggered before he is knocked down, but that's not always the case. He can be floored suddenly while exchanging or while leading with left or right. Or, when off balance, he can be dropped with a comparatively light punch. But when a staggered fighter is floored, he is more liable to be counted out than the victim of a single punch.

An experienced boxer will remain down for the count of eight or nine, so that his head will have time to clear before he rises to face his confident opponent. If the floored man fails to regain his feet before the count of ten, he loses the bout. Or, if he has been knocked through the ring ropes and he fails to re-enter the ring before the count of ten, he is also considered counted-out.

If a staggered and helpless fighter is being battered mercilessly by his opponent, the referee will intervene and stop the bout in order to save the groggy man from injury, even though he still is on his feet.

During the contest, watch closely whether either contestant is using rough tactics—thumbing in the eye, heeling an opponent's face with the glove-laces on the palm of his hand, butting with the head, or hitting below the belt. Each of those " tricks " is a foul.

In the United States a boxer cannot lose a contest on a single foul—only on disqualification after repeated fouling and after warning. In England the decision as to whether the blow disqualifies the boxer is left with the referee. He would stop the fight, if, in his opinion, it was a wilful attempt to disable, after warnings for similar offences, if the boxer who received the blow was sufficiently hurt to jeopardise his chances.

The referee is also the sole adjudicator of a bout. He keeps the score and gives the decision at the end. In other countries, such as America, there are two or even three judges, but in this country the only other officials are the time-keeper and the inspectors, who have no say in the result.

In England the " point system " of scoring is always used. The maximum number of points a boxer can score in one round is 5. Therefore each boxer can gain equal points for a round, 5 and 5, or one can be a fraction of a point or more behind, say 5 and 4¾ or 5 and 4. At the end of the bout the referee totals the points for each boxer and the one receiving the most points is the winner.

Some American States use the " round system " of scoring. Each official (two judges and a referee, or three judges) decides how many rounds, instead of points, each boxer wins. Pennsylvania officials credit a boxer with a "big" round if he wins a round by a wide margin, and with a " little " round if his margin is small. Those " big " and

" little " designations usually prevent a fight from ending in a draw on any score sheet, even if an official credits each scrapper with the same number of rounds. New York State uses a combination of the " round system " and the " point " system." If the bout is close in rounds on an official sheet, he decides the winner on points.

In making up your own minds which contestant will gain the most points in a round watch for the things that will influence the referee:

(1) Who was forcing the fight? (2) Who was landing the most punches? (3) Was the one receiving the most punches offsetting that disadvantage by landing a few blows that caused more damage than his opponent's many? (4) Who was missing with the most punches? (5) Who was winning in the exchanges? (6) Who was showing the worst effects of battle—face cuts, eye bruises, swollen ears, and fatigue?

Usually, if a fighter is knocked down he loses the round in which the knockdown occurs—but not necessarily. If he is merely caught offbalance and knocked down, it discredits him but little. Moreover, a fighter can suffer a clean knockdown, but give his opponent such a battering during the rest of the session that he will take the round.

If a fighter *slips* to the floor when he misses a punch or when his fast-moving feet skid on a wet spot in one of the corners, the slip is *not a knockdown*, and it has no bearing on the scoring of the round.

You will add to your pleasure at a fight if you keep your own score sheet and compare it later with the tabulations of the officials. Use a simple round system, so that your scoring will be a pleasure and not a labour. Do not try to write anything on your sheet during a round. Keep your eyes fixed on the fighters. That's important. If you glance away from the ring for an instant, you may miss the knockout punch.

Using any kind of blank paper, you can make your own

score sheet like the one below. Describe only the highlights of each round in about three lines, written after the round is finished. Make an " X " at the inside edge of the round in which a fighter is floored, and a ") " at the inside edge of a round in which a fighter is cut. When the bout is finished, you'll have a " quick picture " that should be clear and accurate.

OVER . . .

You can make your own score sheet like this:

SCORE CARD		
JOHNNY BROWN 9 st. 7½ lbs. London.	**EVEN**	**BILLY GREEN** 9 st. 8½ lbs. Liverpool.
1. Forced. Rocked him early with L.H. to chin. Out-jabbed him. Landed R. to body near bell.		
	X	**2.** Rallied. Floored him for 6 with straight R. to chin in midround. Kept after him.
	3. Green hooked wildly first 2 mins. Then Brown rocked him with R. to jaw. Kept after.	
4. Gashed Green's R. brow with L.H. early. Kept jabbing at it. Green landed hard R. cross late.	(	
5. Green rocked Brown with head barrage, but in exchange Brown floored him for 9 with R.H. to chin. Green clinched, covered.	X	
	)	**6.** Rallied. Gashed Brown's L. cheek with straight R. Slipped under jabs and beat Brown's body.
7. Feinted Green into slips and rocked him with hooks and uppercuts.		
8. Had better of several furious exchanges. Green fighting desperately.		
9. Green tired, completely defensive. Bleeding from nose, mouth, brow.	(	
10. Pursued, battered him. Floored him for 9 with L.H. to chin shortly before bell.	X	
7	1	2